Every word contained herein is true but will be
denied in a heartbeat, if necessary, for legal
reasons.

Cover design by: Ben Doughty & Natalie Bleau

For Joe Doughty and the light that never goes out...

PROLOGUE:

I did a bit of window cleaning when I was 19 and I hated it. Who knows...? Perhaps I had improved and acquired a taste for it in the quarter century that had since elapsed but I was sceptical.

In all fairness to John, he was only trying to be nice and his suggestion of a window round was as good as any at a time when it looked as if my continued presence on the U.K. professional boxing scene would be about as welcome as Gary Glitter at a 'Save The Children' concert.

As we drove through the hinterlands of suburbia, through Chorleywood towards Bushey, I nursed a can of Stella in my right hand from which I took regular liberal gulps. John, dapper within the confines of corporate convention, was on his way to work. We might have seemed an odd duo to any random spectator, idly contemplating our connection.

Perhaps I was the alcoholic genius detective who solved all the cases with my unique methods and John was my long suffering straight man...? The chance would have been a fine thing because I had no idea how I was going to solve this case, in which I was, decidedly, the prime suspect.

John made his own hours at the office and suggested we stop at a caff in Watford to grab a bit of breakfast. I have always loved a fry up but couldn't have eaten one this morning had it been lovingly prepared by Aphrodite herself.

That said, it would have been churlish to have kept him from indulging his mid-morning appetite purely because I wasn't hungry. After all, he wasn't the most wanted man on Facebook and peckishness is hardly a crime.

We stopped at a greasy spoon owned by an Italian family of John's acquaintance and sat near the door. He ordered a typical juxtaposition of bacon, sausage, eggs and toast and I ordered nothing, as apologetically as I could manage.

It didn't help my mood when the strains of 'Where Do You Go To, My Lovely..?' emanated from a small radio behind the counter whilst John began to eat and I continued to hide my second can of Belgian lager under the table. If the universe had ever asked a coincidentally moot question then this was certainly it. I felt far from lovely and had no idea where I was going to.

Suddenly, my phone rang. I had come to hate the nagging ring tone and knew it was unlikely to be good news. I walked outside to take the call. It was Gary and his patience and understanding had officially expired.

"You just paid that Jackson back. Where the fuck is my money...? 6 of those tickets were for Matt Skelton and he has got some 'orrible mates...! This is going to social media at 12' O Clock. If the money ain't there, then he'll be coming down and I'll be coming down with him.
Don't fucking let me down...!"

At this point, having settled up, John came outside and I briefly relayed the latest goodwill message from one of around 40 people who had paid in good faith for a ticket to the imminent Kell Brook - Gennady Golovkin fight.
Never a shrinking violet John replied, 'Tell him to bring Mike Tyson down if he likes. Who's Matt Skelton....? A Bedford doorman..."

Essentially, he was right. There was a greater likelihood of Gary coming down with the late Joe Louis as his avenging angel than of the Peterborough 16 getting either the tickets or their cash back in the next few days.
The same applied to Scottish Craig and the Dunfermline 9. The Bromley contingent were off

my back, thanks to the benevolence of an old friend I had phoned with an SOS about an hour previously but I was still over 5k in the hole and out of ideas in the short term.

John drove me the rest of the way to Bushey station and tried to say something upbeat as we pulled up. "You'll get through this," he said simply before plucking £40 from his inside jacket pocket and handing it to me.
I took the money and meekly said, "Cheers,", as I had become so accustomed to accepting money from so many people in denominations great and small at this point.

Having bid my friend farewell, I found the nearest off license and bought some more cans of trusty Stella before heading back to the platform. When you feel this spectacularly wretched, alcohol doesn't fix the situation.
It just makes you feel a little bit better.

Waiting for the next train to Stratford, I cracked open another can when the phone rang again. It was Joey Pyle, the South London face assuring me, "You've just got to front it out, mate. Me and Anthony don't think any less of ya'."
"Cheers, Joey, I'll be ok, mate," I mouthed whilst downing more beer.

Big Anthony, the Irish pharmacy magnate made good, was on the line almost immediately afterwards. 2 calls in a row from people who didn't want to kill me. A result of sorts.

"Listen, mate, don't sweat a couple of grand. We're gonna' make plenty. And STAY OFF the bottle, my friend."

"Absolutely, " I agreed while taking another swig of Stella and making my excuses.

I boarded the train and paced up the length of the London Overground carriage. There were plenty of seats but I never could sit down at a time like this. Same as all those times in the dressing room, gloved up, in full battle array waiting for someone to say, "You're on, good luck...!"

As the train hurtled past Hatch End, I knew I was going to turn the phone off at some point today and sooner rather than later. Things were only going to get worse and, in the midst of the impending storm, I had almost forgotten about the great Michael Spinks and the scheduled dinner in Chigwell 2 nights hence.

That wasn't going to happen either.

It's been well established, after a sufficiently arresting opening, most stories take you back to where it all began.

For my part I'd like to take you back to where it all began to go wrong....

1/ THE LAST TANGO IN DROITWICH
(June 1988)

I'm not going to lie to you. I can't remember the precise location or name of the venue but it was one of those typical smoke filled working men's clubs in the western counties/ Midlands crossover that hosted amateur boxing in the 1980s.

I was convinced I had lost the first 2 rounds but was up off my stool early for the 3rd, doing that carefully studied Ali bounce in the corner. For some reason the song 'Never' by twin female fronted rock band "Heart' was reverberating in my head. An unheroic admission but there we are.

My timing was kicking in now and I had loosened up after getting hit too much in the opening sessions. A coach can yell "Keep your hands up," until he's blue in the face (and mine often did) but I generally boxed better with my hands low.

My opponent, a certain G.Craft from the 2nd Parachute regiment, was good but I was finding my range now and making him miss. Make a guy miss and fire back.... Aside from the administration of the coup de grace, what else does a fighter need to do, really...?

I never found out what his first initial stood for but his noisy throng of fellow servicemen called him 'Geordie' and they became yet more vocal as perhaps they sensed the fight was turning. They jeered as I did the 'scissor kick' step that was basically an abbreviated Ali shuffle but I was in control now. I landed a sweet right hand and knew I'd hurt him as he retreated to the ropes. 18 year old, skinny armed me with the Rick Astley haircut had hurt the muscular, tattooed soldier.

At this point I jumped all over poor G. Craft, bombarding him with one shot after another. Within seconds he seemed to wilt, perceptibly, as the referee suddenly stepped in and sent me to a neutral corner. For a split second, I didn't know if he was stopping the fight or administering a standing 8 count but as I turned around, having reached the nearest white corner, I realised it was the latter.

I was keyed up and ready to move in the for kill (an admittedly unfortunate phrase for anyone who defends the Noble Art) when the third man waved me on and suddenly the bell rang, ending the fight.

I felt exhilarated having had a grown man out on his feet but still thought I might not have done enough. But as we came to the middle of the ring for the announcement of the verdict he certainly looked like the loser, with heavy bruising and discolouration over the right eye.

And then came the words that always triggered a euphoria that only those who have experienced it will ever understand: -

AND THE RESULT OF BOUT NUMBER 14..... A UNANIMOUS DECISION... MARTIN IN THE RED CORNER......!

At this moment you feel ten feet tall. You love the other guy as you embrace and tell him how tough and strong he is. You love the two strangers in his corner as you walk over to them in the traditional sportsmanlike protocol of shaking hands and receiving a pat on the back and perhaps a symbolic squirt of the spray bottle.

And you love everyone who came to support you. And they love you. As the old Philadelphia middleweight, Teddy Mann, once said, "If the feeling of defeating an opponent in the ring could be bottled and sold it would make somebody a billionaire."

On this particular night, my modest contingent of support consisted of my best friend 'Drac', his younger brother 'Nance' and a fellow Roxburgh House boxer called James Molloy.

Tony Marlowe, the bumbling but desperately loyal head coach brought me over a pint of lager, whilst I was still getting changed. It was last orders and we would soon need to climb into the minibus and make our way back to Stroud.

At this stage of the game, I had yet to acquire my prodigious appetite for booze and gave the pint to 'Nance' who was a couple of years underage and would appreciate it more than I needed it.

If anyone present that evening had told me it would be 15 long years before I fought again, I'd have told them to lay off the crack, smack or any other fabled poisons I had yet to discover.
But that's precisely how it played out.

2/ LOCK IT UP
(July 1988)

I didn't expect them back this early. In fact, I could have sworn they weren't due home until the weekend. Regardless, I knew that as soon as Derek discovered I had picked the lock and was entertaining the usual suspects in the lounge it would 'kick off' and no mistake.

Even if my Dad had stayed with my Mum in everlasting matrimonial bliss, it wouldn't have been unusual for a teenager to be at loggerheads with parental rule. Throw in a stepfather who didn't really like you in the first place and you had the full apparatus of a war zone.

My Mum, Derek and my younger brother, Seth, had all gone on holiday for a couple of weeks while I had elected to stay home. Clearly, the powers that be were not wildly excited at the idea of me being in sole tenure of the family home for a fortnight and so they attempted to impose a sanction.

'Brooklands', in the wonderfully named Paganhill district of Stroud, was a spacious 4 bedroomed house with attractive green acreage attached. Since my closest friends Drac, Jim and Nick all lived in more petite suburban homes, it was the hang out of choice amongst our little clique.

Derek, in his infinite wisdom, had identified the VCR machine as the cornerstone of our social lives and elected to stash it in the marital bedroom, to which he had newly fitted a lock. He was quite the handyman and presumably thought that confiscating the video player would curtail any late night teenage gatherings in his absence.

In direct opposition to such terrifying effrontery, we picked the lock and liberated the VHS player, probably before my folks even got to Heathrow. The plan was to put it back in place before they returned, although I was tempted to leave the damn thing precisely where it was in a gesture of open defiance. But, either way, I didn't expect them back at this moment.

The interesting thing about the design of Brooklands was that it was built into a hill and most of the rooms, including the lounge, were upstairs. Derek was the first to appear in view. He saw Drac, Nick and Jim seated on one of the living room sofas while Neil and Jenny were sprawled on the other. I was already standing up, anticipating the inevitable showdown.

I had been waiting to smash his head in since I was about 10 years old so perhaps the moment for that epiphany had finally arrived. But as he took stock of the mutinous situation from the landing with my mother and brother bringing up the rear, I could see that, whilst he was far from happy, he didn't want a physical fight.

"Tell me this isn't so, Benjamin...?! How did you get into our bedroom...?"
I muttered something about having a 'master key', although I have no idea why.

"Give me the master key," he demanded.

"There isn't one, " I admitted, "I picked the lock."

He looked at the assembled throng and said, "Ok, everybody leave NOW..."

Clearly, he meant everyone except me but I opted to take him literally as I headed for the staircase and beckoned for my clan to follow. Without further prompting, we filed down the stairs, out of the front door and trudged along the stony driveway towards the gate bearing our domicile's name. Be it a futile effort to call my bluff or not, Derek stood in the doorway and warned, "If you leave now then you don't come back."

"Fine with me," I shot back as we continued our mini exodus through the gate and up the steep incline toward the surrounding suburbia of Mill Farm Drive and Marling Crescent. To place the scene in context, the class of Archway '88, myself included, were currently waiting on those all important A' Level results ahead of some big decisions that would shape the rest of our lives.

Leaving home, with no contingency plan, down to an essential difference of opinion over the preferred location of a video recorder was the last thing any of us needed.

But, aged 18 and a half, that is precisely what I had done.

3/ WINE, WOMEN AND SONG
(August 1988 - December 1988)

Ultimately, I blame Axl. And to a lesser extent, I blame Slash.

The atmosphere as Guns N' Roses took the stage, second on the bill at the Monsters of Rock Festival, Donnington Park was unlike anything I had previously experienced. Two young men lost their lives that day in the stampede near the front and one of them was a kid of my age, rather comically named Alan Dick. Except there is nothing comical about getting trampled to death at a rock concert.

W Axl Rose, with his supreme vitriol and swagger was the Caucasian rock idol to challenge my hitherto unrivalled devotion to Muhammad Ali and Sugar Ray Leonard. They have both long outlived him in my romantic affections but I was 18 and the so called 'Most Dangerous Band in the World' spoke to me.

Slash, with his top hat, low slung Les Paul and unruly hair once described as 'a nest of hissing, seething vipers' was the perfect foil and I was strangely impressed by his claim to drink a bottle of Jack Daniel's a day.

I don't want to sound trite but something happened to me on that fateful day, August 20th, 1988. Not nearly as fateful as it was for poor Alan Dick and his lesser known confederate but my life was forever changed, nonetheless

Jim and Nick were with me alongside another of our recently graduated sixth form mates, Jason Girling. But I knew they weren't 'getting it'. They were just suburban teenagers who liked a bit of 'Heavy Metal.' This wasn't going to knock them for six and steer them away from any remotely normal life path, forever.

Instantly, I had aspirations outside of the Spartan remit of a fighter. I wanted to sing and play guitar and wear make up with an acceptably macho androgyny whilst finding myself knee deep in musician hungry bimbettes. Naturally, I fancied myself as the singer and centre of attention but that Gold Top Les Paul looked pretty cool, too.

The 'live fast, die young' ethos seems awfully attractive at an age when you don't feel as if you will ever die and my sudden infatuation caused me to dig out some iconic predecessors to these latest 'Toxic Twins' from Los Angeles.

It seemed that Jagger and Richards plus Tyler and Perry had gone to hell and back in a pantheon of substance abuse and lived to tell the tale with a wry smile and millions in the bank. Not so much Jagger, actually, but the sentence wouldn't have worked without him.

The point was that boxing had been all that mattered since January 1980 but now I aspired to something else.

In the meantime, while nursing dreams of rock stardom, I was working in a wine shop opposite Stroud Subscription Rooms by the name of Centurion Vintners. After leaving Brooklands I had initially gone to stay at Nick's parents' house for a couple of weeks and it was during this time that I received the A' Level results that so disappointed my mother. I had scored a D in English Literature, a D in Theology and had failed History altogether, which was ironic given my latter status in boxing circles as an encyclopaedic source.

Despite applying to 5 universities, I had only received an offer from 1. Thinking about it retrospectively, my reference must have been atrocious. Admittedly, I had become a bit of a nuisance by the time I reached the sixth form but I'm assuming you don't need to know every last detail of my adolescence.

Liverpool had agreed to accept me on the condition that I attained 2 Bs and a C. Since 2 Ds weren't much good for anything besides the Double Diamond cider logo and I had no inclination to look for a last minute polytechnic placement, I opted to take what I referred to at the time as 'a year out.'

Soon after the confirmation of this scholastic failure, I went to stay at Drac's house which he shared with his Mum and 2 brothers. The wine shop gig was the first job I applied for. Whether the proprietors were inordinately impressed with me as a candidate or had simply taken on the first school leaver who was grateful for the princely sum of £75 a week is unclear but here I was in my first adult position.

The owner was an old boy called Dominic and he was a prick. His second in command was a guy called Bob who was also a prick. The day to day manager, Roland, was an altogether more interesting individual and we bonded quickly.

Roland was 34 and extremely conservative in appearance but in the mid to late 70s he had been the bass player in an Avant Garde punk rock outfit called Gloria Mundi. I was hugely impressed by that. In the pre internet era, a record contact was like some kind of 'Holy Grail' and here I was working with somebody who used to have one and had rubbed shoulders with the likes of John Lydon, Sid Vicious and The Clash.

Drac's mum was awfully decent to me, despite the feeling that she had always vaguely disapproved of my friendship with her son and dinner was always waiting when I got back from a day's work. It was with her help that I found a flat share at the top of town in the converted old workhouse called Stone Manor. If that description sounds somewhat austere, it was actually a rather palatial residence that would have cost millions of pounds to rent in London.

My landlord, Steve, was an affable fireman who used to be in the R.A.F. His claim to fame was somehow cheating death when he fell several hundred feet out of the sky having jumped from a plane, dressed in a gorilla suit, when his parachute failed to open. The other tenant was a bloke called Dave who had a Midlands accent and did whatever he did for a living.

With a flat and a job plus carte blanche to do what I liked outside of working hours (somewhat subject to the aforementioned sum of £75 a week) I felt suitably grown up at this point. My role at Centurion Vintners was neither taxing nor scintillating but I was surrounded by alcohol, for which I was acquiring a taste, and the many hours spent discussing music and life with Roland made it more than bearable.

In fact, with Nick and Jim having moved away to University and Drac already displaying the signs that would see him become a latter day recluse, much of my social life suddenly revolved around Roland. Nothing too wild, admittedly. Just 4 or 5 pints in the Duke of York or the Fleece over innumerable conversations about The Beatles, The Stones, Punk Rock and the vagaries of women

This was all well and good but I hankered for the hedonism and excess that I read about on a weekly basis in Kerrang Magazine. It seemed that you had to be in a band to experience such delights but, the more I broached the subject, I began to realise that Roland had inexplicably missed out in that regard. He'd been the introverted bass player, along for the ride. Not the ambiguously sexual Rock God out front, negotiating the frenzied advances of a thousand female admirers. I was going to have to go this one alone.

Given the title of this chapter that has yet to make mention of any woman besides Drac's mum, I consider it appropriate to tell you that I had my first serious sexual relationship at 16. Her name was Karen, I met her in lower 6th form and she helped me jettison the burden of virginity on November

22, 1986. It happened to be the same day that Mike Tyson knocked out Trevor Berbick to usher in what Jim Lampley called 'a new era in boxing.' Indeed, when I met Tyson, 28 years after this landmark event in my young life, I felt the need to tell him about it.

Karen and I did our thing for several months in what amounted to a crash course in the emotional manipulation and anguish that boys and girls or men and women so readily bring to one another's lives. By the following summer, we were no more.

For a long time thereafter, my sex life bore no resemblance to the fabled conquests of Iron Mike. Having got out of the traps relatively quickly, I had expected the mysteries of womankind to unlock themselves for my pleasure and perusal but aside from a second base here and a third base there (forgive the American terminology), the home run wasn't happening.

Admitting that I had made a mistake wasn't my strong suit but it did occur to me that most of my mates were now in exciting new cities surrounded by hundreds of nubile young women and endless possibilities. And here was I in the snug of the Golden Fleece with Roland, nursing a pint of Waddington's and talking about my plans to take over the world.

Not that I was about to get stuck in a rut. Fate would keep me moving.

4/ YOU'RE FIRED
(December 1988)

In early December, I turned up for work one morning to find Bob behind the counter and Dominic looming on the shop floor. For much of the time, Roland and I had the store to ourselves but either one or both of these pricks would grace us with their presence a few times a week and today was Roland's day off. Dominic wasted little time before getting to the point.

"Ben, this may come as a surprise to you but we don't think this job is really.... you... So we're going to give you a week's notice starting this morning."

It was hardly the most crushing blow but throughout my life I have often experienced a delayed emotional reaction to perceived personal slights and here was no exception. I shrugged and asked if he meant that Saturday would be my last day of duty. He nodded affirmatively before making a few backhanded remarks, insinuating that I generally hadn't risen to the task and perhaps the job in its entirety was too challenging for me.

I felt nothing but contempt for the sanctimonious old cunt as I knew I hadn't conspicuously underperformed but I suffered the rest of the day in his midst and got on with the job. I would be deservedly released from various posts in the years that followed but, on this occasion, it seemed genuinely unfair.

I still had a week to serve, of course, and such disrespect was never going to go unpunished. At the time, I had limitless energy for retribution in the form of practical jokes, wind up phone calls, unwanted pizza deliveries and other more elaborate ruses directed at anyone whom I thought deserving.

With a little help from my friends, usually Drac, I would harass my former employers for many weeks after my dismissal with one wind up or another but the most comical incident occurred on the day of my last shift.

For some time now, Centurion Vintners had been on the market and I knew this because Roland had told me as much. Consequently, I thought it might be a wheeze to have Drac turn up at the shop, posing as a potential buyer, representing some agency or other. When it came to such things, he never needed asking twice although I did wonder if the brevity of his summers might make the whole charade rather unbelievable.

In the event, I was underestimating Bob's abject stupidity. Without so much as a precautionary telephone call to make an appointment, Drac rolled up on the Saturday lunchtime in one of his Dad's old suits, wearing a pair of Clark Kent spectacles and carrying a leather briefcase saying , "Hello, I've come about buying the shop."

He looked like that kid from 'The Inbetweeners' on an underage booze run but silly old Bob Petersen had no resistance to the notion that here was a bona fide executive businessman who was interested in buying a wine shop. Even the given name of 'Martin Urgency' didn't set off any alarm bells, if you can forgive the irony.

Trying not to make eye contact while maintaining a straight face, I offered our visitor a cup of tea or coffee, as I might have done under normal circumstances. With the deadpan expression that was part of his genius, Drac enquired, 'Do you have any Coke, young man...?" I went to the fridge and handed him a cold can of Coke. Bob looked a tad uncomfortable with this departure from protocol but he ushered 'Mr. Urgency' upstairs towards the office, regardless.

As they disappeared up the creaking staircase, Roland quietly expressed his concern that the whole prank might prove absurdly transparent and backfire on me. Be that as it may, it was a bit late for second thoughts. The two of them remained in the office for over 10 minutes although neither of us could properly hear what was being said. By the time they filed back down the stairs, the shop was liberally full of customers as per normal on a Saturday afternoon. With an audience now in place, Drac was ready to put the crowning glory on his performance.

Suddenly, he strode across the shop floor and picked up a random bottle of Soave before shaking his head and proclaiming, "Cheap foreign rubbish.... We couldn't have THIS...."

Returning the offending vintage to its rightful place on the shelf, he suddenly produced a small notebook then fixed his gaze on a magnum of C tes du Rh ne and muttered, "Low grade French piss…" He scrawled in his miniature almanac, as if to make it a matter of record.

Ad libbing, he descended the steps leading to the lower deck of the store and began theatrically stamping on the floor and intermittently prodding the walls. He now had the undivided attention of the assembled shoppers and Bob was compelled to ask what on earth he was doing...?

"I'm testing the structure," he snapped impatiently before proclaiming, "I mean, the whole place looks like it's held together with bloody SELLOTAPE."

While hardly the alpha male, even Bob wasn't standing for any more of this nonsense.
"I'm sorry, but I've given you the courtesy of seeing you without an appointment. I really think you should go now and consult with your partners at the agency and get back to us."

Back on the upper level now, Drac stood near the entrance and said, "Oh, we WON'T be coming back, Mr. Petersen. I find your mode of business incompetent and, If I'm honest, you have been a complete DICKHEAD throughout this entire negotiation..."

And with that, he was out of the door, leaving a visibly crimson Bob Petersen laughing nervously as he became aware that an appreciably long procession of customers had witnessed the scene.

"Sometimes you have to bite your tongue," he said to nobody in particular before jumping behind the counter to assist with the backlog. Roland smiled covertly as If to say, 'You told me so...'

Honour had been defended. New pastures beckoned.

5/ CAREER OPPORTUNITIES
(Dec 1988 - March 1989)

I needed a new job and I needed one fast. Rent didn't pay itself and signing on the dole was still an anathema to me. My mum had raised me to take a dim view of any able bodied person who chose to be a sap on the state's resources, although I would more than make up for any reticence in that regard, latterly. So I worked for a week in a Cheltenham clothes store pretentiously called 'Concept Man' and hated every second of it.

Thankfully, I quickly landed a job as a sales assistant for the music chain 'Our Price.' Younger readers won't remember the brand but in the 80s they were as big as HMV. Second only to being in a rock band, and it's important to remember that I had yet to learn a single chord, this was my dream job.

A dream job that started with a day's training in London, near the BBC studios in White City on what happened to be the same day that Roy Orbison left this mortal coil. At the time, I didn't know Roy Orbison from Roy Castle but I do remember an American chick who worked for the company telling the assembled recruits that a rock n' roll legend had passed. Retrospectively, it's strange to imagine myself never having heard of Roy Orbison because in the next several months I would devour rock history with the same zeal that had made me a boxing historian by the age of 12.

The training concluded and I started work the next day in the Gloucester branch, 9 miles from Stroud. The job itself basically consisted of selling records (vinyl and CDs), assisting customers, managing stock and placing orders. In the course of these duties you could wear whatever you damn well pleased and listen to any music that took your fancy, within reason.

It was the perfect place to harness my newfound passion and delve into the back catalogues of Hendrix, Bowie, The Stooges, MC5, Soul, Reggae, Hip Hop or the more Avant Garde acts like Devo and Television. The 2 shop managers were young and cool. With one notable exception, my co-workers were young and cool. I was young and cool (or at least I was trying to be cool) as were the bulk of our clientele. It would surely take an idiot to mess this one up.

During this period, my sartorial style altered radically. At the wine shop I was still required to look conventional and non - threatening but in this new environment an alternative aesthetic was practically part of the job description. I was free to indulge the glam/punk/ metal look espoused by my beloved Guns' N'Roses and the likes of Hanoi Rocks, Motley Crue and a thousand imitators. I was growing my hair, although it seemed to be taking its damn time and I had reason to be nervous about that from a genetic point of view.

Wandering around Stroud, more interested in beer than bag work, I would bump into old mates from the gym, like Gaz, Geordie or Tony Marlowe himself. They would seem vaguely perturbed by my black clothes, long coat, bracelets and cowboy boots. They would remind me of my astonishing fistic potential and urge me to get back in the gym and cut all of this nonsense out before it was 'too late.' I nodded politely and made the right noises but basically took no notice.

It was also during this period that the burden of the cost of living truly dawned on me. Previously I could walk to work from home but now I had to get to Gloucester and back, 5 or 6 days a week. Budgeting has never been my strong suit and so it wasn't long before I became adept at the subtle art of fare dodging. In fact, I proffered every possible excuse within the scope of human experience for not having a valid ticket until the regular train guards positively hated me.

Sometimes I would carefully alter the date on a ticket with a biro or perhaps the aid of scissors and glue. A plethora of typically implausible emergencies were often relayed to rather sceptical ticket inspectors and there was always the option of hiding in the toilet or pretending to be asleep. Admittedly, the latter two ruses were not nearly elaborate enough for my taste.

It just so happened that Drac had gotten a job in the Gloucester branch of Debenhams around this time, so we frequently became partners in these various deceptions. One good scam was to offer to pay with a £50 note, as the guard invariably wouldn't have sufficient change, which allowed you to travel free of charge or recriminations. This was obviously a limited option that was entirely dependent on either one of us having a £50 note in the first place.

One morning in early February' 89, Drac's luck ran out and he got nicked on the platform at Gloucester station. As the Old Bill were carting him off, he had the misfortune to be seen by the assistant manager of his department although unbeknownst to him at the time. Having called in with a standard excuse he turned up for work the next day only to receive his marching orders. Mickey Duff was right about loyalty and dogs.

In my case, the process was more formal but amounted to the same thing. After a 3 month trial period, the managerial hierarchy at Our Price had elected not to offer me a permanent contract.
I could see their point. My time keeping wasn't brilliant, I played hard rock and heavy metal on a permanent loop and I simply wasn't a very good worker. I probably wouldn't have offered me a contract either.

It was time to plot my next move and, like a many a young man with delusions of grandeur before me, I opted to head for 'The Smoke'.

6/ RICHMOND HEIGHTS
(March 1989 - August 1989)

After my second consecutive reversal in the world of work, Mum suggested I come back home for a bit. When I say home, the family had moved from Stroud by now and relocated to Burton on the Wirral. Back to our roots, essentially, since I was born in Birkenhead Hospital and spent the first 8 years of my life in Wallasey. Derek was away on a saddlery course and said he would feel better if there was another man in the house while he was not in residence. I should probably have politely declined but, instead, I agreed and headed North. It didn't take too long for me to realise I had made a mistake.

Having lived on my own, in theory an adult, for almost 9 months, I was even less suited to living 'at home' than I had been previously. Despite the evil stepparent's conspicuous absence, Mum and I clashed over pretty much everything from politics and music to feng shui. I was young, headstrong and largely unacquainted with diplomacy. Despite being 17 years older than me, she was uncannily similar in the same regard.

The bickering went on for a few weeks until, one day, I could take no more. I was undertaking driving lessons at this time so one afternoon I packed a bag and asked my instructor if he had any conflict with the lesson finishing in Elsmere Port. He had none, so as our session came to an end, I got out of the car and walked to a lay-by adjoining the M56 and started hitching.

Although I would do a lot of hitchhiking in the ensuing years, this was the first time I had ever tried it. I had no idea if this was something that only happened in the movies or a genuinely viable way of getting around on a non-existent budget.
After about 15 minutes of cars going past and a couple of cretins doing the evergreen 'thumbs up' joke, a red Volkswagen Golf slowed down and pulled into the lay-by several feet in front of where I had chosen to plot up.

I was excited in the same way a fisherman must feel at the moment of that first bite and wasted no time in jogging towards the car as its driver opened the passenger door and asked where I was headed.

The man in the driving seat was an affable Irish gentleman in his mid-30s.The charm of hitching besides it's inherently cost effective principle is that you get to talk to people you would never have met, otherwise. You will always get picked up by the odd nutter but most cars that stop are occupied by interesting people who perhaps did a bit of hitching themselves in younger days.

It took me precisely half a dozen lifts to get to Stroud, where I hung out for a couple of days catching up with friends. Spring was in the air and it was nice to see the usual suspects again but I didn't want to stay. Now that I knew hitching actually worked, It wasn't long before I found myself standing beside the road leading to the A419, soliciting any random conveyance to London.

I lucked out when my first lift, a white Austin Metro driven by a young man scarcely older than myself, took me all the way to Heathrow. He was en route for a flight to Madrid and grateful for some good chat as he traversed the M4. After one more lift from a tradesman in a white van I had reached the Chiswick exit, characterised by that neon Lucozade bottle that continually poured itself into a glass on the side of a factory wall. It's not there anymore, alas.

It was a short walk to Gunnersbury station after which I bunked the district line train two stops to Richmond where my Dad lived. My parents had split up when I was 5 and I don't recall seeing much of my him until I was 10 years old. Thereafter we had enjoyed an idyllic relationship, very much based on our mutual love of Boxing. Richmond had always represented a kind of Utopia for me.

In my earlier teens he would take me around all his favoured local watering holes, introducing me to a surfeit of colourful characters, some of whom would not have been grossly out of place in an episode of 'Minder.'

What I didn't realise at the time was that Dad had no desire to share his living space with anyone. Not even his son and heir, as he frequently referred to me. My dad, Joe Doughty, was an alcoholic. Ask any recovering alcoholic and they will tell you it's a progressive illness. In his case it was a progressive illness that saw me find him dead in a sea of bottles and cans in mid-December 1997, a few days before Prince Naseem Hamed fought Kevin Kelley at Madison Square Garden.

But in the spring of 1989, he was an alcoholic who preferred to prop up the bar of the Red Cow or the White Horse, harassing the more conservative patrons with his acerbic wit and impromptu fashion critiques. He wasn't exactly Britain's best dressed man but if he saw somebody in a blue suit with brown shoes then he felt compelled to make them aware of their sartorial folly. Which usually resulted in some kind of skirmish.

He rolled his eyes as he answered the door at 14 Mount Ararat Road, with a faint smile that said, 'So, it didn't work out at your mother's then...?' He seemed to enjoy it when things went wrong, particularly where his ex-wife was involved. The one significant development during my abortive 6 week spell at Mum's was that she had bought me a cheap black electric guitar and a tiny portable amp. Aside from a bag of clothes and cassettes, I had turned up on my Dad's doorstep with little else besides the guitar and my illusions.

As I entered the flat, we both filed into the kitchen and he made tea. Dad never seemed to have a kettle but would boil the water in a saucepan. He was idiosyncratic like that and set in his ways to the point of a behavioural disorder when he wasn't drinking. And, right now, he wasn't drinking. I preferred the atmosphere when he was but it couldn't be helped.

One character of my Dad's acquaintance on the Richmond pub scene was a singer and guitar player by the name of Alan Henry. He was originally from Blackburn but lived in a single room above an independent betting shop opposite the Red Cow. Every inch a pastiche of the 70s rock star, Alan also drank too much and seemed to reside in that classic era of rock n' roll, 20 odd years prior to the emergence of 'Acid House.'

Indeed, he played such material in pubs around West London with a guitar wizard named Rob in a duo called 'The Uninvited Guests'. Given the number of times I would see Alan politely asked to leave one licensed premises or another, it wasn't such a bad moniker.

For the next several weeks I spent a lot of time with Alan. Drinking, talking about music and furthering my rudimentary guitar skills. When I say drinking, it was still kindergarten stuff on the scale I would become aware of but perhaps I was sowing the seeds that would lead me into 'the madness' in due course. At this point, I could play a few chords but none too fluently and I found it impossible to sing and play at the same time.

Meanwhile, my Dad was either drinking or else he was not drinking. Both pastimes had their drawbacks in his case. He had no visible means of support yet was able to maintain a nice one bedroomed flat in an historically expensive area of Greater London. In the pub, he claimed to be a commodity speculator but I had no idea what that might involve and never saw any palpable evidence of it.

When he was drinking, he was a lot of fun. Ribaldry and boxing chat were the order of the day. Responsibility and protocol could go and fuck themselves. I'm ashamed of it now but I generally encouraged his drinking because it was in drink that I spent the true quality time with my father.

We bonded during these endless sessions from one barstool to another, when his guard was lowered and we made up for lost time.
Throw in the old axiom about the apple never falling far from the tree and it seemed unlikely that I would ever be the one who would lead him to the temperate society.

When he was sober it was a different story. Sometimes he might be in a good place but, at worst, he was like a man in purgatory. Battling depression and living the kind of monotonous existence that might have made a nun seem frivolous.

It was during these spells that he desired to be alone. Certainly, the last thing he needed was his 19 year old son sleeping on the sofa, cranking out 'Appetite for Destruction' while fussing over his hair in the mirror. Hair was a moot point, in fact, because my Dad didn't have any. From the age of 17 he had experienced quite radical hair loss and photographs from the early 70s show him glabrous domed with incongruously long hair at the sides.

Since 1978 he had worn a very convincing hairpiece and reinvented himself with a new peer group in Richmond. Bearing in mind that my childhood memories of him were fuzzy, I didn't initially realise he was wearing a wig until it became detached one night after a drunken collision with the radiator in the master bedroom. I was horrified at the sight of him prostrate and exposed.

In any case, he only wore the wig for the sake of appearances. When indoors and in the melancholy of abstinence, he liked to be bald in his own company. Consequently, he made an effort to ship me out to Clapham where he had encouraged me to get a live in bar job at a pub called the Coronet.
I started on a Friday and was fired on the Monday.

The daft Irish bastard who had been entrusted with the task of breaking the bad news took me to one side and said, "Ben, we've had a chat about your attitude and dress and... well, were not terribly pleased, to be honest with you, so we'll have to let you go this morning." On the plus side, he paid me for the 3 shifts I had done, so I grabbed my bag and guitar and headed back to Richmond on the train.

Upon arrival, I walked into a pub opposite Richmond Station called The Orange Tree and happened to find my Dad in there drinking with an old character by the name of Eddie Brooks. There was a copy of the Daily Mirror on the bar and, for some reason, the headline read 'SACKED...!' I quickly explained to them both that it was rather pertinent in my case. I might have gotten a brief lecture in different circumstances but everything was treated with frivolity in the pub.

When it came to jobs, I was now 0-3 in boxrec terms although I had left Concept Man of my own accord so perhaps we could call that a draw.

It was a sunny day and the old man was wearing a pair of psychedelic beach shorts and one of my old Def Leppard T-Shirts. As always, he thought he was carrying it off but Eddie was probably closer to the mark when he said, "You look like a right cunt, Joe..." Regardless of how he might have looked, he was stuck with yours truly again for the foreseeable future.

The beauty of the situation was that, when he was drinking, he was glad to have me around. And so off we went on one of those beer soaked odysseys from the Orange Tree to the Sun, to the White Horse to the Black Horse, to the Red Cow to the Belvedere, to the Mitre and the Marlborough to the Duke's Head. The best benders occurred on what he referred to as 'Nameless Tuesdays.' Basically, ordinary working days when you weren't really supposed to be on the sauce.

There was too much anticipation around weekend drinking and too many regular people getting out of their brains. On a Nameless Tuesday session, you could look at life and reflect. There was a magic about it.

That's why I liked drinking with my father and was invariably happy when he fell off the wagon.

7/ SHAKE SOME ACTION
(September 1989)

Perhaps we should recap...? I was 19 years old, unemployed, sleeping on my Dad's sofa and learning to play the guitar. I didn't have a game plan beyond those bare facts but was increasingly aware that I hadn't had any action with the fairer sex for an unacceptable amount of time.

There was Debbie, the Irish chick who pretended to miss the last bus home after a few drinks in the White Horse but that had been a while ago. Reclining on a couple of sofa cushions laid on the hard floor whilst my Dad slept in the next room can't have been the stuff of her fantasies but that's life.

However much a person might love music, the free availability of adoring pussy is a major motivational factor for any young heterosexual man who gets involved with a band. I didn't have a band as yet but alcohol has facilitated many a sexual encounter and it was about to come in handy once again, although not in the way you might imagine.

I was on an all day session with Alan Henry in the midweek as we ricocheted between the Red Cow and the White Horse, no doubt strategically. The two pubs were very close together and it took 30 seconds to walk from one to the other. Indeed, it was part of local folklore amongst my old man's crowd that on one Saturday evening he had been asked to leave the

White Horse and mistakenly believed he had relocated to the Cow when in fact he had walked into the lounge bar of the same establishment. When he saw the landlord, a self important man known as 'Treacle' (because that's what he called everybody else) still standing there he is reported to have said, "For god's sake, Treacle, HOW many pubs have you got in Richmond...?"

In the White Horse, Alan always drank Pride and Pride. That's a half pint of London Pride on draught and a bottle of Pride in a pint glass. "Pride and Pride, COLD bottle," he would specify in his Lancashire tones. The drunker he got the deeper his voice became and the more insistent he was about the cold bottle. I did drink pints but my tipple of choice at this time was Jack Daniel's and Coke because that's what Slash drank, or so he said in Kerrang. Years later I would only ever drink liquor at home because pub measures simply weren't strong enough.

In any event, as we imbibed our respective poisons, Alan told me of his plans for the evening.
He was going to visit 'an old tart' in Acton. In the course of his regular pub gigs, Alan met a lot of bored housewives and single mothers in need of diversion and a degree of carnal satisfaction. He said I was welcome to tag along provided I understood that "at some point I'll be taking her off for a good shagging and you'll have to sleep on the sofa." I had nothing better to do so I told him I was in.

We still had a few hours to kill so, inevitably, we got more drunk. Of the two of us, he was visibly the drunker. This was partly because he was much further down the line of alcoholism than I was and also because I found it quite easy to stay on an even keel drinking Jack and Coke.

At about 7pm we left the bar and headed to Richmond station to catch the overground. When you're drinking, time flies. I suppose that's part of the charm in an altered state where a simple journey from Richmond to Acton can become an epic adventure, fraught with potential danger.

On this occasion, we reached our destination without incident, although Alan didn't look too clever and was starting to slur. For such a small, relatively insignificant place, Acton has an inordinate number of train stations named in its honour and I honestly don't know if we got off at East Acton, South Acton, Acton Town or Acton Central. Nonetheless, we were soon making our way through a maze of suburban streets and terraced houses in the West London dark.

They say that a sudden introduction to cold air can have an adverse effect on a drunk person. In support of this theory, Alan's gait was demonstrably woeful by now. It was as if a mutiny was occurring within his own body and every muscle and synapse had resolved to act independently. I began to wonder precisely how well this woman would receive us in view of the condition he was in.

When we arrived at the appropriate house and Alan pressed the doorbell, a moderately attractive woman in her mid-30s with shoulder length dark hair answered the door. She engaged in the pleasantries and welcomed us indoors, not appearing to be perturbed by my presence. I'm tempted to use the spare prick at a wedding analogy but it would be all too apposite.

Aside from immediately requesting another drink, Alan's first undertaking was to censure Maxine's choice of apparel. It wasn't every night that an affordable, if rather drunk, facsimile of Ronnie Wood knocked on your door and she was hardly dressed for the occasion as far as he was concerned. I was a little surprised to see her dutifully scurry to the bedroom in order to get changed but that's precisely what she did before returning to the living room in a black dress that had buttons at the front from the hem to the neckline. The second outfit met with his approval.
"That's more like it, ' he said as she smiled and replied, "Sorry...! I was still in mummy mode."

Maxine played the good hostess and ensured that we were ok for drinks before putting on the Stones' 'Steel Wheels' album, presumably for Alan's benefit. Struggling for coherence, he continually made reference to the buttons at the front of her dress, suggesting that they ought to be undone and then he passed out, face down on the sofa.

To her credit, Maxine was a pragmatist who clearly believed in the old maxim that the show must go on. She was in the mood for what might have been her monthly dose of R and R and seemed perfectly grateful for the availability of a willing young reserve.

I was never a huge advocate of the 'beer goggles' alibi but I was drunk enough to fancy this average 'housewife' in a sexy black dress as she reclined on the carpet while Mick Jagger assured me that I wasn't the only one with mixed emotions. Was I perhaps in two minds out of loyalty to my friend who lay comatose on the couch...? In all honesty, I had no such reservations. Earlier in the day, he had referred to her as 'some old tart' so I wouldn't be scuppering any wedding plans.

Picking up where Alan left off, I asked if the buttons on her dress were functional or purely for show. Putting down her glass of Chardonnay she asked, "Why don't you find out...?" Having gotten the green light, I leaned closer, put my hand on her midriff and we kissed. Within 20 seconds of this ritual, she was rapidly liberated from the black dress and relieved of her bra so I could suck her breasts as we sprawled across the living room floor. Typical teenager technique, 100 miles an hour off the blocks.

A potential sprint was prolonged by Maxine's sudden sense of propriety. The proximity of Alan, albeit sound asleep, prompted her to say, "Let's go to my room, " as she picked up her clothes and cut Mick n' Keef off in the middle of 'Rock And A Hard Place.' We bundled into her bedroom while she switched on a lamp and lay on the double bed adorned with a lilac duvet and white pillows whispering, "Good things come to him who waits." I took that as a signal for me to slow down and as we climbed between the sheets, I suddenly thought of Tony Marlowe, my old Boxing coach.

I was 12 years old, in the back of a minibus, coming home from a show in Yeovil and Tony was lecturing some of the senior lads about the pleasures of the flesh. "We enjoy sex more than you youngsters because we can make it last," he boasted. The handful of lads in their early 20s on board the bus laughed but I was starting to think that dear old Tony must have been right. Not necessarily about making it last but that it must surely get better. Sex with a person that you are not really into can be a strangely detached experience. Here I was, banging Maxine but thinking about Tony Marlowe.

'The sooner this bitch has an orgasm, the sooner I can go to sleep' was all I was thinking. Actually, no, I was also thinking of being back in the pub and telling the story of how I had heroically stepped up to the plate when Alan was too drunk to service one of his paramours. But the old adage that urges caution when speaking of the Devil seemed rather apt as there were suddenly clear and audible signs that he was beginning to stir in the front room

Maxine had good instincts and immediately darted into her young daughter's room. Perhaps she was in the habit of this kind of farce. Not 10 seconds after she had made her exit, Alan entered the room, still pissed, and began to undress. He patted me on what he thought was her arse and said, "I'm here now, baby."

"Glad to hear it, ya' bloody lightweight," I retorted. It was dark but I could see the confusion on his face as he attempted to unravel this conundrum. "You're joking...?!" he blurted. I had no idea what he thought I might be joking about but the best explanation I could muster was, "Maxine gave me the bed. She's in the other room," The realisation having sunk in that it wasn't his lucky night, he shuffled out of the room. I assume he went back to the sofa but I really don't know.

The next thing I was aware of was daylight and Maxine coming in with a cup of tea and a knowing smile. She kissed me on the cheek and lay the cup down on the bedside table saying, "Morning, honey." She was getting ready for the school run but also talking to a friend on the phone in the hallway. As I sat up in bed sipping my tea, I could hear her saying, "Hilarious...! They're both still here, I'll tell you all about it later."

Soon, I was dressed and ready to get on my way. I said goodbye to Maxine but didn't wait for Alan or ask for her number. I was glad to have ended the drought but had no desire for an encore.

8/ BIG BAD WORLD
(October 1989 - March 1990)

Dad was in one of his excruciating sober periods which meant he wasn't out and about carousing in the pubs. Accordingly, my drinking and socialising continued to orbit around Alan and the regular Richmond haunts. One Sunday afternoon, in the lounge bar of the White Horse, we bumped into some acquaintances of his that I hadn't met before.

Rob, Alan's opposite number in The Uninvited Guests, also played guitar in what you might call a proper band called the Gabriel Set, fronted by former teen punk rock star, Andy Blade. In 1977, Andy had been the singer in a barely pubescent four piece named Eater and he was most enduringly famous for chopping up a pig's head live on stage at the Roxy.

Actually, I didn't know any of that at the time but he had an air of stature and bohemian cool, sat at the traditionally more salubrious end of the pub with this stunning young wife, Emma, plus long time friend and rock photographer, Ray Stevenson. Upon invitation, we pulled up a couple of chairs and I quickly became engrossed in this new company.

Alan was a laugh and he could carry a tune or pull the odd bird but we didn't have what you might call an intellectual connection. To my 19 year old provincial sensibilities, these people were interesting. Not so much Emma, she was just young, vibrant and hot but Andy and Ray had either written books or appeared in them and seemed to know everyone from Bowie to Billy Idol on a personal basis.

Andy was immediately attracted to me because he always kept a keen eye on plausible young talent. I don't mean that he was gay, far from it. Blade was heterosexual to the point of lecherous but he viewed any reasonably intelligent, good looking young man with the right aesthetic as a potential 'wing man' and maybe an addition to the band. I was attracted to Andy because he was older, wiser and seemed to have already lived much of the heady existence that I was desperate to experience: Gigs, girls, drugs, travel and that all important degree of fame and notoriety.

Ray was a more conservative character, as befits a man behind the lens, but a witty and likeable presence, nonetheless. I thought of Roland who had hitherto been my marker for authentic punk rock lineage. Roland was a wonderful person but his involvement in the big picture was marginal. Andy had been at the cutting edge with the in crowd.

As antiquated as it may sound, in 1989 pubs would still shut at 3pm on a Sunday afternoon and open again at 6pm. Accordingly, this seminal meeting was curtailed by the bell and Treacle's familiar exhortation to 'COME ALONG LADS, PLEASE...''

We said our goodbyes before I took a stroll back to Mount Ararat Road to see if Dad might have moved from his chair in front of the TV since I last saw him. Given that Andy and Emma only lived around the corner from my Dad's flat, I'm surprised we didn't meet earlier but I would bump into him with increasing regularity from here on in.

Another person I met through Alan who happened to be a good friend of Andy's was a guy called Chris, an appreciably middle class gentleman in his mid-30s who lived within spitting distance of the White Horse. Alan had phoned from the pub and invited him for a drink one evening, chiefly because we had run out of money and Chris clearly had a few quid 'wrapped around him.'

His position as managing director of a company that made state of the art mixing desks placed him in a healthy tax bracket in an era when you couldn't simply turn your bedroom into a digital recording studio with a lap top and a couple of apps. . Furthermore, as a confirmed gay bachelor, his outgoings were less than the burden of a traditional family man.

Chris had a hopelessly recurring habit of falling for young straight boys and I was about to become the latest in a long line of endlessly chaste crushes. He didn't fit any stereotype of being overtly camp or excessively well dressed and couldn't warm to the gay scene. Consequently, he fell in love with one young heterosexual man after another and they were often musicians. I couldn't call myself a musician as yet, although I looked the part, but Chris turned out to be a brilliant guitarist who had played in bands and done the bohemian thing before joining the rat race.

The following Sunday after my initial meeting with Andy, I was back in the White Horse with Alan, Chris and an Austrian couple who had come to visit Alan, for whatever reason, and spoke very little English. After a couple of rounds, Chris invited the throng back to his pad for a drink and a smoke so we finished up and repaired to the one bedroomed flat that he had inherited from his mother.

It was a simple but tastefully furnished abode with Chris's collection of guitars being very much the focal point. Stood to attention like obedient soldiers in the front room were a Gretsch, a Les Paul junior, a Fender Strat, a telecaster and a 12-string acoustic. Only a small sculpture of a naked man gave any clue to his sexual proclivity. Perhaps I had expected manacles and rough trade, in my innocence.

Chris put on some music (I later found out it was 1970s folk artist, Roy Harper) before fixing a couple of vodka and cokes and handing out beers. Then he returned from the kitchen with a large lump of hash and sat down to roll a joint. I suppose this constituted my entry into the world of narcotics and a disappointing one at that. As the spliff came around to me, I took a few drags and waited for a palpable effect but didn't feel any different ten minutes later. In retrospect, it seems more than likely that I wasn't 'taking it back' but I was never able to acquire a taste for weed, despite subsequent efforts over the years.

Before long, the telephone rang and it happened to be Andy on the line. Chris was due at Andy and Emma's for a late lunch and had to make his excuses. He came into the lounge and politely informed Alan and the Austrians that it was time to leave. Then he turned to me and said, "You're invited for lunch."

"Who is...?", I asked.

"YOU is...!" he replied, pointing his finger in a manner that struck me as mildly flirtatious, although I may have been oversensitive to the possibility.

Andy and Emma lived around the corner in Kings Road, not to be confused with the more iconic street in Chelsea that is associated with the birth of the Sex Pistols. As we arrived, Emma was busy preparing couscous and chicken while Andy entertained a dotty, affluent sounding woman of 30 something and her older cockney boyfriend who had shades of what I would come to call a plastic gangster. Clearly, Andy liked a diverse cast of characters in proximity while he ate.

Unsurprisingly, the soundtrack was of crucial importance and something that the host controlled exclusively, constantly getting up to change the record or insert a new tape. And so we dined and conversed to the strains of The Smiths, Aztec Camera, The Only Ones, T-Rex and The Lilac Time.

As the wine began to flow, I was very aware of feeling that this was the kind of company I belonged in. I was a small town boy who had been in London for less than 6 months and Andy represented the gateway to a new world. He was funny, intellectual, talented, had impeccable taste in music and a hot young wife. He also appeared to have indulged all of those chemical and carnal delights that I was keen to throw myself at the mercy of. I wasn't interested in Alan Henry's hungry Acton cast offs. I wanted to snort cocaine from the navels of naked Canadian girls in Parisian penthouses. In time, I would but we must not get ahead of ourselves.

We passed several hours around the dinner table in the large open plan room that also encapsulated the kitchen and lounge until everyone was pleasantly drunk and it was decided that we should venture back out to the pub. As we were leaving, there was a brief skirmish between me and the plastic gangster, who misinterpreted a quip I had made and had obviously been brooding over its implication for at least an hour.

He asked if I was 'having a pop' at him while stressing that 'Nobody does that to me." Thrown by my alternative appearance he seemed taken aback when I asked if he wanted to go outside and make something of it. But the situation was quickly appeased by cooler heads and we shook hands and headed into town for more drinks at the Cricketer's on Richmond Green.

At the bar, Andy covertly apologised for having such an individual in our company and admitted he had never met the guy before. He seemed impressed by the way I'd been prepared to stand up for myself. Being as Andy would do anything to avoid a physical altercation, the notion of a bohemian with muscles appealed to him. At around 10pm we called it a night as I headed back to Mt. Ararat Rd with the full body armour of pleasant inebriation. Dad was still sober but didn't seem to be enjoying it very much. It occurred to me that he might just as well have a drink.

From here on in, I saw less and less of Alan and more of Andy and Chris. It's no exaggeration to say that Andy became something of a guru to me for the next couple of years and he was as happy for a protege as I was for a mentor. He had a large, eclectic social circle and introduced me to a surfeit of interesting characters, many of whom had a back story in the music business

Street cred and charisma aside, it was his song writing that truly had an impact on me. Andy Blade may have been a 16 year old punk rock idol belting out cerebral 3 chord masterpieces like 'No Brains' and 'Get Raped' but in the ensuing 12 years he had grown beyond recognition into a sophisticated songwriter who had, nonetheless, retained his punk swagger and pop sensibility.
He showed me how to write a song and why you should write one in the first place. Of course, nobody can really tell you that but it would be years before I found my own voice.

In the midst of these seemingly innocuous but life changing coincidences, my paternal and maternal grandmothers both happened to die within a week of each other at Arrow Park Hospital in Liverpool.
It was a strange time but provided an olive branch for me and Mum as we hadn't spoken since I had acrimoniously departed from Burton. For his part, Dad

decided to spend his 13 grand inheritance on a 6 month excursion to Australia, leaving me in the flat. Well, actually, he didn't voluntarily leave me in the flat at all. He did his best to ensure that I lived anywhere besides Mt. Ararat Road in his absence but fate conspired against him.

I'd heard there was a room for rent at Alan's place, above Graham Taylor's the turf accountant, so I told Dad I would be moving in there but the deal fell through for whatever reason, leaving me temporarily homeless for the first time of many.
The flat was vacant but I didn't have a key so I went to stay with Chris for a week whilst considering my next move. He seemed more than happy to have me around for a few days and was becoming increasingly fond of me but not so fond that he desired the arrangement to become remotely permanent

Chris commuted to Oxfordshire every day in the week as that's where the office was based. I would usually hang about the flat watching MTV and helping myself to the odd beer or glass of Jack Daniels although I wasn't a big solo drinker at the time. I also got in some invaluable guitar practice with the ample choice of 'axes' available but I knew that I couldn't allow the grass to grow under my feet.

After a week had elapsed, I took the short walk to Mount Ararat Road and told the landlord, who lived upstairs, that I was supposed to be house sitting while Doughty Snr. was away but he had forgotten to leave the keys. To my astonishment, he let me into the flat and gave me the keys although he made no attempt to hide the fact that he was far from elated at the idea of me being in the property unsupervised.

Regardless, the flat was now mine for several months and I was free to hang around with my clever bohemian friends, with little in the way of responsibility besides the obligation to sign on every two weeks.

Drawing the dole was no longer a taboo, despite my conservative upbringing. I had read about too many bands who subsisted on government handouts until they made it big. 'Making it big' was an inevitability I took for granted since Melody Maker and the NME never interviewed the thousands of aspiring rock musicians who fell by the wayside.

I did work for one day during this period, in an upscale wine shop in Turnham Green called Hunter and Oliver. It was
a fledgling company with affluent pretensions and due to my charm and eloquence, the management appeared to view me as a fantastic addition to the team. Perhaps I would have been had I not gone from my first shift to watch Andy play a gig at the Mean Fiddler, before getting pissed at the after party and never turning up for work again.

Clearly, I was too special and heroic for regular employment. My genius needed time to ferment. How was anybody supposed to write the definitive album of a generation while simultaneously stacking shelves in a Chiswick off license...?

Frankly, it was beyond me.

9/ THINKING OF THE USA
(March 1990 - August 1990)

Although he was on the other side of the world in the pre-internet era, Dad soon found out that I was living in the flat but didn't appear to have a problem with it. He phoned me intermittently to discuss whatever big fights had taken place. Leonard - Duran 3 and the seismic shock of Buster Douglas destroying Mike Tyson's aura of invincibility in Tokyo. He was obviously having a whale of a time having started in Coolangatta and worked his way through Melbourne and Sydney and I could tell from the frivolity of his tone that he was drinking again.

He'd managed 6 months without a drink before he left the UK but when I asked for confirmation that he was off the wagon he said, "Yeah, but it's DIFFERENT here."

In AA circles they call it 'geographicals.' The thought process in which an alcoholic imagines that if he simply relocates to another part of the world then perhaps he will be able to drink with less disastrous consequences. But it was hard to put an entirely negative spin on this sun soaked relapse because he was blatantly enjoying himself, in sharp contrast to those months of housebound abstinence.

I still saw Alan from time to time and still had a key for his place that he'd given me when we lived in each other's pockets. One evening in mid-March, I decided to pay him a surprise visit. He didn't have a landline phone anyhow and nobody had a mobile, although they probably just about existed in primitive form.

Spring had yet to kick in so it was dark but for the streetlights as I stood outside his front door on Sheen Road and inserted the key. For some reason I was having trouble turning it and so my left elbow protruded at a right angle as I tried to open the door. As I struggled with the lock, I suddenly felt something solid collide with my elbow and turned around to see what Andy would have called a 'lad' glaring at me with a mixture of confusion and malevolence.

He had clearly been on the sauce or else he wouldn't have banged his head on my elbow in the first place. As ever, I didn't want any trouble, so I said, "Sorry, mate."

He glowered at me and said 'WHAT...?!"

"Sorry, mate." I repeated.

I'm pretty sure he must have heard me but, once again, he shouted, "WHAT...?!"

I was losing patience already.
"Sorry about that, mate, but it was probably your fault, to be honest."

"My fault...? Ow's it MY fucking fault then...? I 'fink you're a wanker anyway. The way you're dressed."

To place this gauntlet in context, he was dressed like a typical 'beer boy' who drank in the Black Horse and probably lived near the lower Mortlake road. Jeans, shirt and brown leather jacket. I was wearing black PVC trousers, an Aerosmith T-Shirt with a cut off denim jacket, cowboy boots and an elaborate purple silk scarf. The time for arbitration was over. With his reference to onanism and the quite unsolicited sartorial barb, he had lit the fuse as Nigel Benn might say.

He squared up to me.... I immediately nailed him with a right hand that landed flush above his left eye. It was 'off'....

I followed up with a left hook and then grabbed him in a headlock, ramming his skull into the betting shop window. Not hard, just to assert my authority over the situation. At this point a black guy who had been waiting for a bus came over to get a closer view of the unscheduled entertainment. Playing to the gallery somewhat, I dropped my hands and dared my half cut adversary to take his best shot. He swung a few times and missed as I peppered him with counters and encouraged the poor sod to try harder.

Poor sod is about right as I was beginning to feel a bit sorry for him. To receive this kind of schooling from a bloke in eyeliner and PVC trousers must have seemed like a bad dream. Opting for a change of tactics, he placed his right hand inside his jacket, as if to imply he was concealing a knife, and said, "C'mon then... Ave 'anuvver shot at me..." I didn't believe he had a weapon but saw it as sign of surrender. On the street, it was always my M.O to establish superiority and leave it there. I never wanted to hurt anyone and couldn't ever bring myself to stomp a man on the ground or use a 'tool'.

I told him to "Watch your manners next time and you won't get hurt," before turning my back and reinserting the key in the door.

"If that's the way you wannit," he warned, "I know where you live... I could get the firm down 'ere."

"Course you could, " I replied.

The lock appeared to have been lubricated by the proximity of violence, so I opened the door and ascended the two flights of stairs to Alan's room. It seemed appropriate to mention what had just taken place outside and, true to form, he scolded me.

"Ben, don't have fights outside MY door. What If they do come back...?" He recovered his sense of machismo quickly enough to say, "I mean, I'm not worried about myself but I've got a lot of expensive equipment in here."

I assumed he was referring to the PA system that made The Uninvited Guests a commercial viability in the beer houses of Chiswick and beyond. Before I could explain that the altercation had been regrettable but unavoidable there was a knock at the door. Not expecting guests and naturally vigilant, Alan peered out of his window and saw that there was a squad car parked outside. Never mind 'the Firm' this guy had gone squealing to the boys in blue. Since the Richmond Constabulary had never been noted for their fairness and diplomacy, he pushed me into the bathroom and told me to lock the door while he went downstairs to deal with the situation.

Alan answered the door. The two officers informed him that the drunken young man in the brown leather jacket with the large swelling over his left eye was alleging that he'd been assaulted and had seen his assailant enter the property not 5 minutes ago. He feigned surprise and invited them to come inside to search the building but insisted that the drunk man in the brown leather jacket must remain outside as he didn't know him from Adam.

The other two tenants, Glen and 'Torquay Peter', were out so Alan exhibited their empty rooms before taking Good Cop and Even Better Cop to his own room on the second floor to prove that it was clearly devoid of other occupants. They were about to leave when one of them noticed the closed bathroom door and asked, "Whose room is this...?" Thinking on his feet, Alan suddenly knocked the door and enquired,

 "Are you still in the bath, Sal...?"

It occurred to me to respond affirmatively in a girlish voice but I opted to say nothing. Being accused of looking like a girl was one thing, plausibly sounding like one was another. Growing in confidence he said,

"My girlfriend's in there getting changed. I've got to take her out in half an hour."

That was good enough for these two fine bastions of law and order. They headed back down the stairs, apologising for the inconvenience.

"Sorry to trouble you, sir. This bloke's a bit pissed."

He was both pissed and rather unimpressed with their investigative prowess, it was fair to say. Outside, I could hear him shouting, "I fuckin' know e's in there. I just seen 'im go in wiv' a key...!" Politely, they told him to chalk it up to experience and get on his way.

As I opened the door, we both grinned and breathed a collective sigh of relief as Alan said,
"I tell you what.... You're the ugliest bird I've ever taken out...!"
'That's not even true, " I laughed as he suggested we go across the road to the Red Cow for a well earned beer.

I thought it was too soon after the incident and 'The Cow' was too close to the house so, instead, we swapped jackets and I ran up the road to Chris' flat having told Alan I would see him at the pub in an hour.

In 1990 it was much more common to knock on a friend's door unannounced and Chris was perfectly happy to bust out the Jack Daniels as I related the evening's events. Sat on the sofa with a drink at my feet, I excitedly demonstrated the punches I had thrown 15 minutes earlier whilst seeking to explain why I had arrived wearing Alan's jacket.

Chris made an observation. "I've never seen you this animated. I think you enjoy it.' He was right, I did enjoy fighting. More crucially, I missed Boxing. Pretending to be a rock star in an affluent part of

Surrey, surrounded by older friends who had vaguely been there and done it, was never going to be a sufficient surrogate for the adulation and excitement of the ring. At that moment it occurred to me that I couldn't just hang around, waiting for Dad to get back and hoping Andy would parlay me into some kind of stardom in the meantime. I wanted to see the world and sow my wild oats.

Actually, I had been planning a trip to Sydney, several months before both grandmothers died and the old man had decided on his own jaunt Down Under. Before he left, he had entrusted the sum of a thousand pounds to my mother with instructions to give me the cash when I had proper travel arrangements in place. But, lately, I had been thinking about going to New York. I had typically romantic visions of making my way from 'The Big Apple' to Los Angeles in classic 'Road Trip' fashion but hadn't given much thought to budgeting and logistics.

"I think you should travel," he agreed, "And I would recommend you go to Sydney. New York can be a dangerous place."

It was a waste of breath telling me to avoid potential danger. I always considered it a challenge. He might just as well have booked me a flight to New York there and then. And, essentially, he did.

"If you DO decide on New York then I'll give you a free return ticket next month, "he casually announced.

"Why would you do that...?" I asked, still ever so slightly suspicious of this older gay man. With a smile that said, 'Calm down, kid, you're not THAT cute,' he replied, "Because I get stand by tickets to the States all the time through the company."

It made a lot of sense to me. I didn't precisely know what a 'standby' ticket was but why pay for a flight to Australia if you could go to America for nothing...? My mind was made up. I was going to New York and already had a free return ticket and a thousand pounds spending money. Actually, I would leave Gatwick with considerably less than the dollar equivalent of a grand but that's another story.

I stayed for about an hour and then thanked Chris for his impromptu hospitality and the imminent gift of free passage to the promised land before heading back down the road to meet Alan. He had been stone cold sober when I left him but was now was bordering on paralytic. He was one of those drunks who turned a corner on the flip of a pint glass and morphed into an entity that bore no resemblance to the jovial Northerner that he was in temperance. In his case 'Pride and Pride' came before a fall.

He was drinking with a bloke called Dave who I had seen around Richmond, intermittently. He sounded South African and was definitely not a hundred percent sane but always seemed to have plenty of money to buy copious rounds of drinks.
It was hard to imagine him being in gainful employment, so I assumed he had either inherited money or was in receipt of some substantial state

benefit in exchange for whatever was wrong with him. Dave got another round in and handed me a pint of Young's lager while Alan brought him up to speed with the highlights of the evening.

"Fuck me, you must have smacked that guy, Ben. His eye was out here, " he said gesticulating appropriately.

I was still on a high but didn't fancy staying in the Cow. Alan was only going to repeat himself on a permanent loop and wasn't above becoming abusive or importuning some young lady or other so I finished my drink and told him that I was expecting a phone call from my Dad back at the flat.

I wasn't expecting a call from my Dad.
And neither was I expecting what happened next.

10/ WAIT TILL YOUR FATHER GETS HOME
(August 1990)

I had been living the fabled life of Riley, albeit on a giro budget, and my attitude towards domestic household maintenance was extremely relaxed.
I figured that I was the same as any other 20 year old male in that respect, despite being so different and special in every other aspect, obviously.

I would routinely rise at midday, have a quick shower, put on whatever Rock N' Roll regalia I saw fit before fixing my hair and heading to the pub.
That usually meant The White Horse although sometimes I would arrange to meet Andy at the White Cross down by the river.

As stated, I didn't have a lot of money but you can always drink if you truly put your mind to the task. In Kerrang Magazine it was called 'ligging' and I would become a '7th Dan' ligger, in due course. Somehow, I would either stay in the pub all day or else wind up at a party cum social gathering at the house of somebody in the extended peer group. Andy and Chris' flats were the staples and former Sex Pistols engineer, Dave Goodman, also threw some colourful parties.

Either way, I would generally get back to the flat after midnight and decide it was time for guitar practice. I had no qualms about playing loud electric guitar between 12 and 6am before eventually falling asleep on the sofa, despite there being a perfectly sumptuous bedroom available. I figured that Axl and Slash would more than likely have been sleeping on sofas when they wrote 'Welcome to the Jungle' and I was guardedly suspicious of luxury.

As for the neighbours, I wasn't exactly disrespecting them while I created this relentless nocturnal din. It simply never occurred to me that anyone would object in the first place.
Remarkably, nobody ever did complain directly but there was an amusing postscript on that score.

14 Mount Ararat Road was a 3-tiered property. The landlord lived on the top floor, as befitted the moral high ground he occupied. On the first floor lived an Italian couple. Despite the compulsory nightly updates on my development as a musician they remained stoic and never said a word in protest.

Then, at some point, these Latin lovers vacated the flat and returned to their homeland. I had pretty much forgotten about them until the day I received a small package from Italy containing a tiny toy synthesiser with an accompanying note that read, 'For playing between 12 and 6am, please. HA HA...!' I had to hand it to them, that was quite funny but this constitutes a digression and I was about to tell you what happened next.

It was a Tuesday morning and I awoke with a start on the sofa as I heard someone entering the flat and then immediately saw the unmistakeable form of the old man looming in the doorway. He was wearing a baseball cap and that rather abhorrent shell suit that he seemed so inordinately fond of.

Casting an eye over the copious debris that seemed to engulf the living room including 3 guitars, an amplifier, a stack of Rock magazines and a surfeit of unwashed cups and dishes, he shook his head woefully before saying,

'Don't ever got to go to Bangkok if you can help it..."

We were uncannily alike in many ways but his borderline obsession with tidiness was the glaring exception to that general rule and he clearly wasn't impressed at the abject state of his former sanctum. He was obviously about to tear a strip off me so, as much as I wanted to know what was precisely so inclement about Bangkok, I opted to go on the front foot, taking umbrage at the lack of notice ahead of his return.

"You didn't TELL me, man...!" I remonstrated whilst sitting up in my sleeping bag.

"I shouldn't have had to tell you ANYTHING. Look at the mess of this place...! You've got some work to do, " he assured me.

The conversation went back and forth for a moment or two but the crux of the matter was that I had precisely an hour to get the flat looking ship shape and pristine. The 'carnage' was largely cosmetic, when all said and done. After getting dressed and moving a few objects, washing the dishes and running the vacuum cleaner around, Chez Doughty was looking perfectly fit for human habitation.

When I flipped the mattress in the master bedroom before putting on a new sheet, I noticed two porno mags had been stashed underneath and wondered why I had never found them before. Nobody is comfortable with the notion that their parents are sexual beings so I quickly banished any visions of paternal solo gratification from my mind and continued with the task in hand, if you will forgive the expression.

Within less than an hour, he was happy with the new aesthetic and said, "We may as well go to the Duke's for a pint."
It was his grizzled way of saying, "I love you, son. It's great to see you again."
It sounded like a good idea to me and so off we went to the Duke's Head around the corner.

"The two GREATEST rock idols of their generation reunited again...'" shouted Jerry the bar man as we entered the Duke's, a typical Richmond regulars' pub literally a stone's throw from the flat.
Jerry was one of my Dad's best mates and a very popular figure in their mutual drinking community. He had dark hair, styled in a somewhat 70s fashion and was slightly over what body fascists might have considered to be his ideal weight but so charismatic and gregarious that it didn't seem to matter.

Jerry worked at the White Horse for many years but had recently switched to the 'Duke's' for whatever reason. The landlord was an Irishman by the name of Pat Dalton, or "Dalters' as my Dad called him. To his credit, he was one of the more tolerant local proprietors when it came to the old man's ribald behaviour with a drink in him.

We ordered 2 pints of lager plus a burger with chips each and, after mandatory updates and banter with Jerry, the freshly sore subject of Bangkok was duly addressed.

It turned out that he had met a chick in Coolangatta and they were sufficiently serious about one another to make a pact to return to London together. The flight itinerary included a one night stopover in the Thai capital and therein came the stumbling block he explained. Like so many of my Dad's stories relating to anything that happened when he was drunk, it sounded a tad sensational.

Essentially, he claimed that any expectations of romantic bliss were cruelly scuppered when his new love interest stumbled upon 5 Thai prostitutes in the hotel room they had booked for the evening. Since the old man had entered the room some minutes earlier, it would seem he had been tarred with guilt by association.

Or so he claimed. Certainly, he wasn't the type of man to go with a 'brass' (or 5) so whatever actually happened, ,his version of events involving a misunderstanding with an overzealous street pimp who had asked if, "You want ladee...?" seemed as credible as anything else.

It also seemed safe to assume that the incident owed a great deal to their mutual consumption of alcohol but the upshot was that 'Deb' had got the hump and boarded the next available plane back to Sydney.

My selfish reaction to this tale of romantic woe was one of causal relief. I tried to picture the scene that had unfolded scarcely an hour ago but with the addition of a woman I had never met before tentatively auditioning as my new stepmother. It would surely have been awkward.

After a couple more pints we took a stroll down to the Red Cow and then across the road to the White Horse where we drank until closing time.
Such days were of purest gold as far as I was concerned. As you will know by now, the old man wasn't always persona grata in either hostelry but the old axiom about absence making the heart grow fonder seemed to apply. The regulars were pleased to see him again and some were interested in his tales of 'derring do' Down Under.

There will always be people who are not interested in such tales, as any man with the testicular fortitude to walk on the wild side will discover upon returning to his natural habitat. It's not that they are actively disinterested in your stories so much as the inability to comprehend anything beyond the snug parameters of their own lives.

But I wanted to hear the stories and had a few of my own to swap. I was also keen to show off my burgeoning guitar skills, purchased at the expense of the regular sleeping patterns of the Italian couple on the first floor. In the meantime, we drank and talked until Treacle's familiar call to make ourselves scarce could no longer be credibly ignored.

Upon arrival back at the flat, a combination of jet lag and inebriation propelled him to the master bedroom while I sprawled on the sofa, as usual.
He would continue to talk about his erstwhile Aussie flame for a while hereafter but, to the best of my knowledge, they never met again.

11/ BAG IN THE USSR (August 2 - 3 1990)

Shortly after 10am the next day, he strode into the front room with the exuberant vanity of a man still half pissed from the night before. Dad didn't get regular hangovers but generally woke up imbued with a comical mania.

Eyes affably glazed and rubbing his hands together theatrically, he half shouted, "RIGHT...! When does the boozer open..?"

Given that he was perfectly au fait with the UK licensing laws, I took it to be a rhetorical question. Nonetheless, I saw fit to ask a stupid one of my own.

"Are you going back on it today...?"

"Well, I've GOT TO, haven't I..?" he said, hamming it up and throwing his arms aloft. On further reflection, he added, "I'll tell you what...When Richmond gets a beach, I'll come off the piss.." He appeared to be suggesting that going on the piss was the only viable course of action for any vaguely sensitive man in the face of such bland urban monotony.

One might imagine the scene unfolding against a drab autumnal backdrop but it was the height of English Summer. He was right about the glaring lack of a beach, though, and I was agreeable to any train of thought that favoured gratuitous drinking.

Boxing had been my sole sense of mission since the age of 10. Without it in my life, there was simply nothing I would rather do than go on a bender with the person to whom I felt most akin. I'm almost making it sound as if my ring career had been cruelly cut short due to injury or some other fateful circumstance. Of course, I had tossed in the towel of my own free will, preferring to nurse the fanciful illusions that were born that fateful afternoon at Donnington Park. Music changed my life. Too late would I realise that it was probably changed for the worse.

We got ourselves together and made the short walk down the road to the Red Cow, just as it was opening its doors for commercial trade. The first two pints of Young's Premium went down like mother's milk as we sat on high stools at the bar.

Dad always sat, or more commonly stood, at the bar. In his absence, I had gotten used to sitting at a table as that was how Andy liked to hold court. In a suitably exclusive comer, away from the 'riff raff' of working class men who liked a bet and talked about football. But the old man had to be near the action. At the bar, he could be privy to every rumour, joke or conversation about matters of import. During 'downtime' he could always flirt with the barmaid and, crucially, he remained in constant proximity of the next drink.

As the second pints of Young's were duly served by a nubile entity called Sharon, it seemed as good a time as any to tell him about the standby ticket and my plans to go to New York.

He knew Chris by sight from the White Horse and had heard that he was gay. The old man was basically a libertarian who hated racism and wasn't avidly homophobic. At the same time, he had always hung with a typical 'man's man' type of crowd and was almost certainly unacquainted with the kind of bohemian 'gay friendly' joints that I would come to know in the course of my travels.

In any case, he thought the New York venture was a good idea. He thought everything was a good idea when he was drinking and that was precisely why I was so fond of this version of him.

In abstinence he could be so bloody negative. I use the term abstinence rather than sobriety because I would eventually learn that there is a veritable chasm between the two states of being. But the best part of 3 decades would pass before that wisdom was purchased at considerable expense.

Within an hour, Andy walked into the pub, seeking a well deserved libation after the taxing rigours of his morning window round. If I have hitherto painted a picture of an artist who existed on an ethereal plain then I should probably mention that he also did a bit of window cleaning to make ends meet. He seemed to regard it as a necessary crucible in order to quell suspicion from Emma's less charitable relatives who thought he was only after her inheritance.

Blade had always kept his distance from the old man, assuming he was one of those boorish Richmond louts, who got their worldly information from the 'Red

Tops' and didn't like 'poufy' musician types. Nonetheless, I made the introductions and an instant bonhomie was established.

The ale was flowing and it was mutually agreed that we should move across the road to the White Horse. Therein, the conversation revolved around 70s bands and the punk rock revolution. One drink lead to another and the next time I looked at the clock it was 10pm Everything was fine and dandy until Dad's impromptu rendition of 'Paranoid' was suddenly challenged by a group of Welsh Rugby fans at the bar who broke into their sovereign anthem without warning.

"I HATE NATIONALISM...!" Dad shouted a little too loudly for Blade's liking or comfort. The tension was increased when he stood up and began to sing along with this amateur male voice choir in mock parody:

"OH.. THE LAND OF MY FATHERS...
IS A LOAD OF COBBLERS...."

Predictably, the Welsh contingent took umbrage at this flagrant disrespect and things might have gotten physical had Treacle's wife, Sheila, not come over to our table and asked if we wouldn't mind leaving, terribly. I grabbed hold of the old man and escorted him off the premises via the saloon door with Andy in hot pursuit. It was a shame to miss last orders but It could have been worse and at least nobody got barred. An early night beckoned.

I awoke around 9am the next morning and got straight on the phone to Virgin Airlines. The gentleman on the other end of the line explained that, with a standby ticket, a passenger must be ready to travel at any moment a seat became available. He added that there were currently no flights to New York on that basis for at least a week but, naturally, the situation was subject to change at any time, in which case they would call me without delay.

I put on my 'Guns N' Roses Live At The Marquee' cassette which had the desired effect of getting the old man out of bed. "What's that blasted racket, treacle...?' he asked while traipsing into the lounge with a broad grin. The enquiry was entirely jocular and that was a good sign. It also meant that he would be drinking again today which was vastly preferable to the immediate alternative.

I've already alluded to the fact that Dad didn't get ordinary hangovers. What would happen is that, around 2 and a half weeks into a bender, he would suffer an indescribably dreadful comedown. At that moment, whatever had previously been regarded as funny was suddenly devoid of all humour.

He would spend the first day swathed in a blue towelled bath robe and an ungainly sense of self pity, shivering in front of the electric fire and intermittently retching into the bathroom sink. Such misery was always compounded when he reflected on the collateral damage to his bank balance, incurred during the period of revelry.

Since he had only been back in the country for two days, it was impossible to assess the duration of this current bender but it was clear that the whole world wasn't going to come crashing down today and that was reason enough to be upbeat. As he went into the kitchen in search of cloudy lemonade to quench that frenzied morning after thirst, the telephone phone rang.

It was Simon from Virgin Airlines asking if I wanted to fly to Newark, New Jersey 'tonight at 9.15pm'.
I told him, 'Yes, I'll take that...' and after getting a few more cursory details, I hung up. Dad looked at me expectantly and enquired,

"They've found you a flight...?"

"Yeah, tonight at 9.15..."

He seemed excited on my behalf.

"How do you feel NOW...?" he wanted to know.
I didn't like being asked how I felt and simply shrugged, "Better get packing, I suppose."

After I had packed a large holdall and got my documents together, we went to the Red Cow for lunch. My imminent departure had changed the tone of things and what might have descended into typical carnage was suddenly a more civilised affair. I would need to be at Gatwick for around 7pm and, accordingly, I had arranged to drop in on Andy and Emma at 5pm for farewell drinks and bon voyage.

By this time, they had moved from the place on Kings Road, having bought a small flat in Lichfield Court, an exclusive new block above Waitrose. It was very small, in fact, but they had made the most of spatial resources and turned it into their own bohemian love nest.

We sat on the floor, in the manner of an outdoor picnic and toasted my safe passage to the land of the free. It was quite a sentimental moment that made me realise just how close I had become to Andy, in particular, but before long it was time for me to leave and catch the Gatwick Express via Richmond station. At the door, Andy looked at me with a kind of elder brotherly concern before saying, "I hope you know what you're doing..." I assured him that I did before saying, 'Thanks, mate. I'll see you in 90 days.'

The Gatwick Express arrived expressly at Gatwick. I stood in line at the Virgin check in desk and then hung around the departure lounge waiting for flight V93 to Newark. I'd brought the latest issue of Ring Magazine as reading material to help kill the time.

" Birkenhead, eh...?", said an audibly Scouse gentleman as he checked my passport at the gate. I was born in Birkenhead and my passport duly reflected that fact. I was welcomed aboard the aircraft by a blizzard of pristine Virgin hostesses and took a seat by the window. I had been to New York on a family holiday in '87 but making the trip as an 'adult' seemed much more exciting.

I looked at the aerial route map that would always remind me of John Lennon's 'turn left at Greenland' quip and ordered a Jack Daniels and coke. Free drinks were an undeniable bonus to the ardour of the long-haul flight. Despite the narrative hitherto, I had yet to start drinking with any kind of problematic zeal, although I would make progress in that regard over the next few months.

8 hours and roughly the same number of JD and cokes later we touched down in New Jersey at around 11.20pm, local time. The first drama occurred at baggage reclaim.

I stood by the carousel waiting for my blue holdall to appear for as long as I reasonably could before it become apparent there was a problem. At that point, I sought out a representative of Virgin Airlines and informed him that my luggage was a no show. As it turned out, two pretty black girls from London had suffered the same misfortune and seemed a good deal more annoyed about the situation than I was.

The dashing young American trouble shooter assured us that such things happened from time to time and that we shouldn't panic. He asked me for an address and phone number at which I could be reached during my stay in New York.

For some reason, I told him that I was supposed to be staying with a friend in the city but had written his address in my diary, which was still inside my luggage. This wasn't true. It was my intention to check in at the Vanderbilt YMCA in midtown

Manhattan but I can only presume that my story was intended to exacerbate the inconvenience that I would now be subjected to.

"So you will require a hotel tonight, sir...?"

"Absolutely," I concurred, simultaneously astonished at the suggestion. He handed me a piece of paper and ushered me to a shuttle stop from where I could pick up a free conveyance to the Holliday Inn, Newark.

"Just hand over that voucher at reception and you're good for tonight. We will be in touch when your bag is located. I apologise for this, sir."

The shuttle ferried me to the entrance of the hotel, less than 5 minutes' drive from the airport. I checked in with the piece of paper that presumably denoted Virgin Airlines would be picking up the bill and took the elevator to a double room on the 9th floor.

As I entered room 932, it was hard to view the loss of my luggage in an entirely negative light. I had cable TV, a mini bar, 2 sumptuous double beds and an epic nocturnal view of the Manhattan skyline. Provided my bag was recovered in the next couple of days, then its temporary absence seemed perfectly survivable.

This was probably my first major awareness of what people would later refer to as a 'charmed life.' Life on the road was clearly about riding your luck and turning negatives into positives. I reclined on one of the beds, flicking through the TV channels and happened to find a documentary about the great Alexis Arguello. It was the kind of thing that you would never see on British television and served to confirm my romantic notions of 'the promised land.'

Shortly after it finished, I fell asleep. It had been a long day, after all.

12/ NEW YORK (August 4 - 6 1990)

I felt agreeably out of place, eating breakfast the next morning in the ground floor restaurant, surrounded by white American families and executive businessmen. I only had the clothes I sat in, consisting of a pair of ragged denim shorts, a Guns N' Roses T - Shirt and a baseball cap, worn backwards in the style of Axl Rose.

There was still no sign of my luggage and Virgin had duly comped me for another night at the inn.
I was quite happy for the situation to drag on a little longer and decided that a bus trip into Manhattan would be the best way to spend my day while the search continued.

I went back upstairs to the room and called Dad, purely to brag about my relative opulence. Predictably, he was ready to castigate me for what he could only assume was an abject failure to grasp even the basic tenets of travel budgeting before I quickly explained that Richard Branson was footing the bill. Since transatlantic calls have never been cheap and I wasn't sure if I could swerve the charges, I soon hung up.

I caught a bus from the airport to Grand Central Station which took around 40 minutes. A Holiday Inn is a Holiday Inn, wherever it happens to be located, but as soon as I set foot on bona fide New York soil, I expected to feel the same amorous rush that I had experienced on my initial visit in '87.

Ask anybody who spent any time in New York in the 1980s or early 90s and they will swear that it was a lot 'edgier' than the millennial version. The old incarnation of New York City was a roller coaster and people either loved or hated it for precisely the same reasons. As I disembarked from the bus and walked across the concourse, I wasn't disappointed.

Inevitably, there was a degree of self consciousness about it but I really did feel the way I imagined a young Axl Rose must have felt, hitting downtown LA for the first time. And, faithful to the narrative of 'One In A Million', there really was a motley assortment of unsavoury looking black men, covertly advertising their illicit gold chains from behind rolled up copies of the New York Daily News.

As I found my way out of the station and walked down 42nd Street, I was immediately aware of the sheer size of this fabled city. I didn't like to admit it but I was ever so slightly intimidated. The endless mythology around U.S gang culture made me reflexively wary of groups of black males at whom I wouldn't have batted an eyelid had I chanced upon them in Shepherd's Bush or Acton Town.

At this point, I could not safely have been described as 'streetwise.' Most of my year in London had been spent in the watering holes of Richmond, save for the odd trip to Carnaby Street to purchase some shiny black trousers or other items crucial to the maintenance of my 'crumpled glam' aesthetic. I had good instincts and would learn quickly on the job but, at that moment, I didn't know precisely what to do in Manhattan on my own, at 20 years old.

A couple of years down the line, I would simply have found the nearest bar, ordered a beer and let the chips fall where they may but, in my relative naivety, I opted for some random shopping. I bought a hamburger, a T-Shirt and a satirical comic called 'Heavy Metal.' After walking around aimlessly for a couple of hours, I decided to retrace my steps to Grand Central and catch a shuttle back to the hotel.

Shortly afterwards, I was back in room 932 sitting on one of the double beds when the phone rang. It was a gentleman from Virgin with the good news that my bag had been located. Having been erroneously placed on a flight to Moscow, it was making its way to the good old U.S of A as we spoke and would be back in my possession tomorrow.

I spent the rest of the evening relaxing and watching American TV, which still held a novelty value at this early stage. The following morning, I had breakfast before reporting to reception in order to formally check out and pay the phone bill I had incurred when I called the old man. I was already concerned about my threadbare budget, so it did occur to me to leave without settling up but, for whatever reason, I chose to play it straight.

I caught a shuttle to the airport and retrieved my bag from the Virgin baggage reclaim department. I thanked the attractive, heavily made up lady who presented it to me at the desk before unzipping the navy blue holdall to check that it actually contained my clothes and miscellaneous items.

Now it was time to commence this gritty and daring odyssey, without the comfort of a 3-star hotel. I caught another bus to Grand Central and headed for the Vanderbilt YMCA on 34th St, an area that New Yorker's refer to as Midtown.

10 years down the line, I'd have gone to Harlem and checked in at one of the budget hostels in the neighbourhood. But, at the time, I was far too credulous of the stories that portrayed Harlem as an Afro - American replication of war torn Beirut so I opted for the Vanderbilt purely because Julian had recommended it.

I haven't mentioned Julian hitherto but he was a mutual friend of Chris's whom I'd met a couple of times at gigs and gatherings. Julian had also gotten a standby ticket from our smitten benefactor and would be joining me in the Big Apple as soon as he could get a flight. His suggestion that we stay at the Vanderbilt was fine so far as it went but there were a surfeit of cheaper options I'd have favoured had I not been so new to the game.

A rather camp, light skinned black guy checked me in as I paid for 3 nights plus a deposit for the room key. The Vanderbilt was a big establishment that boasted around 800 rooms, more akin to a hostel than a hotel but you got your own room with a television. There were no communal dorms so far as I could tell.

Having located my room on the 5th floor, I endeavoured to make myself at home but soon grew weary of basic cable and opted to venture out in search of diversion. Clearly lacking imagination and confidence, I found the nearest McDonald's and ate a burger and fries whilst eyeing a gaggle of pretty black girls at a nearby table. Their accents and vernacular held much romantic charm for a small town English white boy with libidinous visions of the American negress Aphrodite.

As I walked back to the hostel, I bought a soda for a very young looking beggar who asked, 'Can you buy me a soda...?' before going to bed early. Hardly an epic first night in the Apple when all said and done. Still a tad jet lagged, I dozed off to the relentless noise of metropolitan activity that filtered through the window.

13/ RAY AND THE SMARM KING (August 6- August 12, 1990.)

The next day, I gave Ray a call. Ray, whom you might remember as Andy's photographer friend, spent a lot of time in New York where he shared an apartment in Greenwich Village with a guy called Norman. I used the pay phone in the corridor, dialling the number that Andy had given me and asked if he fancied meeting up for a drink. I was glad to hear him say, "Tonight, if you like...?" I tended to live from day to day and couldn't abide it when people required excessive notice for any social undertaking.

He told me that I shouldn't have any trepidation about using the subway and suggested I come over to his place for around 8pm and we could go from there. I wrote the address on a scrap of paper and hung up.

The evening came and I took a cab to the address on Barrow Street, although I should have heeded Ray's advice and caught the subway. At this rate, my budget would be non existent before the week was out. Having located what I hoped was the right apartment, I pressed the buzzer and waited for a response.

"Hello...?"

"Hi.. Is that Norman...? This is Ben..."

Whoever it was buzzed me in through the main entrance before Ray answered the apartment door wearing only a pair of boxer shorts. "I'm in 'house clothes'...!" he quickly explained with a degree of self consciousness. New York City has always been known for its legendary hot summers and, as I entered the lounge, it became clear that Norman favoured an equally scant attire whilst at home during daylight savings time.

The third member of their household was an attractive oriental lady whose name I didn't catch upon introduction. She turned out to be Norman's girlfriend but the vision of her clad in black, flanked by two white men in their underwear made the whole scene look rather lascivious.

After a quick beer and an update on any essential Richmond gossip, Ray dressed and we took a stroll down to the 'Scrap Bar' on Bleecker Street. It was just the kind of basement joint in which one could imagine the New York Dolls holding court in the mid-70s. Intrinsically, Ray was about as Rock N'Roll as tea and biscuits but he clearly knew some agreeable dives. We drank Brooklyn lager as per his recommendation.

The next place we went to had a 3-piece band playing rock n' roll covers, including Johnny B. Goode. Waiting for service, my eyes fixed on the barmaid's abruptly defined tan lines, her brown shoulders in stark contrast to supremely white breasts, half visible, I mentioned this to Ray who duly declared, "I've never realised how erotic that can look before...!" It had taken almost 72 hours but I was finally relaxed in the ambience of New York City. And the night was young.

We finished up in a place called the 'White Horse' which was undeniably a nice touch on Ray's part. It had been mocked up to look like an English pub, although it bore little resemblance to the Surrey namesake of our mutual acquaintance. To be out drinking at 2.30am on a Monday night was a novelty for me and I was even more enamoured by the idea that we could continue for another 2 hours, if we so desired. It was common for New Yorkers to meet up as late as 10.30pm for beers and conviviality. It seemed so much more civilised than 'Booze Britain' and the mandatory desperation to get tanked up before closing time.

Ray had a relatively early start in the morning so it was decreed that we would get a slice of pizza somewhere and call it a night. It all seemed so ideal. Late licensing laws and pizza by the slice, 24/7. Despite my intention to remain in the States until my visa expired, I had no idea if I was simply passing through New York or would attempt to stay for weeks or months. Ray got by with a bit of photographic work so maybe I could find some kind of cash in hand subsistence.

Pleasantly drunk, I bid my compatriot farewell and caught a cab back to the Vanderbilt. If was as if I was trying to go broke as soon as possible, perhaps believing that only in destitution would my survival instincts kick in. Falling into a heavy sleep, I recalled a Shakespearean quote: 'It is madness but it hath method in it.'

When I woke up the following morning, I could see that somebody had pushed a note underneath my door. I scrabbled across the bed to pick it up and saw it was from Julian:

'BEN, WHERE ARE YOU...? YOUR TV IS ON BUT YOU'RE NOT ANSWERING. I'M IN ROOM 552. I'VE GOT A BOTTLE OF WHISKY...'

Hastily, I threw on some clothes, walked down the corridor to room 552 and knocked on the door. His familiar handsome countenance appeared in the doorway, greeting me with me, "Ben, mate..." before he sat back down on the bed, tossing his enviably silken black hair out of his eyes. Eyes that betrayed a long-haul flight and half a bottle of Johnny Walker Black but, even with a hangover, he was absurdly dashing.

Excitedly, I explained how I would love to have joined him for a whisky session last night but had been out on the 'razz' with Ray, attempting to convey that I knew NYC like the back of my hand already. He lit a cigarette and suggested we get some breakfast somewhere, adding, "You know this city better than I do.. Lead the way..."

We found an agreeable diner a couple of blocks from the hostel and discussed our imminent agenda over eggs, toast and a rather woeful facsimile of what we ordinarily called bacon. His friend Tom was flying into JFK early evening and so we resolved to do a bit of casual sightseeing before meeting him at the airport in a few hours' time.

Regardless of my indefinite plans, Julian was only in New York for a few days before he and Tom headed to Boulder, Colorado to launch his rock star dreams with Mario and the boys. He had met Mario, an American exchange student and virtuoso drummer, during his second year at York University after which the two had forged a friendship and played a few gigs.

Mario lived in Boulder with his English wife, Debbie, and had put together a band for which Julian would be the front man. Julian was a reasonably good singer, although far too 'clean' for my tastes, and knew his way around rhythm and lead guitar. Inevitably, neither of those assets did anything to diminish his seemingly mandatory appeal to the fairer sex as I would discover in due course.

In any case, the plan was to launch the band on the vibrant Colorado campus scene and cut a few tracks in the studio. Julian had only just graduated himself and Plan A was to become a pop star like his idols, Lennon and McCartney. Nonetheless, it was obvious that he already had one eye on a more corporate Plan B. He was going to have a fabulous life whether he became famous or not.

"Listen, mate, there won't be any room for you to stay at Mario's with me and Tom but you're welcome to head out that way with us…" he said whilst taking a drag of his Marlboro cigarette. I said I would think

about it. The truth was that I was nearly out of cash already and had pretty much decided to look up my great uncle Lenny in Illinois.
Either way, any fanciful notions of living in New York would have to wait for a good few years.

For the next few hours, we wandered around Manhattan, taking pictures here and there with our disposable cameras and generally finding merriment in the concrete jungle. At one point it was decreed that I should take a paparazzi style snap of a pair of Hasidic Jews, who appeared comical to our English sensibilities, as they crossed the street. The severe umbrage they took at being singled out for this random 'Kodak moment' made it funnier still.

Our aimless trek included an abortive attempt to locate an old friend of Julian's from a previous NY expedition a couple of years ago. He remembered the address of the guy's girlfriend in the West Village and saw fit to explain, "He's a plumber and a coke dealer." That was all well and good but nobody answered the buzzer and it was soon time to catch a bus to the airport and provide Tom with a fitting reception to the land of opportunity.

I'd met Tom at least once previously on home soil. Like Julian, he was an upper middle class kid from Richmond and seemed nice enough. As soon as he had negotiated immigration and naturalisation, we opted to take a yellow taxi back to the Vanderbilt. The three of us sat in the back of the cab as Tom immediately began to update Julian regarding a recently consummated romance, lowering both his and the collective tone with, "Yeah, I 'jabbed' her, mate..."

That was a new one on me. To the best of my knowledge, a jab was a straight left hand but the metaphor served as an unwelcome reminder that it had been a while since I'd jabbed anyone in either context.

Darkness had encroached by now and the views were typically stunning as we traversed the Brooklyn Bridge into Manhattan. Particularly for Tom, this being his first glimpse of the legendary skyline. He referred to it as 'stylish', in the same context that young people say 'bad' or 'wicked.' It appeared to be a buzz term in the argot that he and Julian shared.

After checking Tom in at the hostel before a quick shower and change, we were ready to hit the town. I resolved to take the boys to the Scrap Bar where Ray had taken me 24 hours previously, although our passage was hampered by geographical confusion.

I thought I knew where I was going but it soon become obvious that we were circling Washington Square Park, engulfed by various predatory looking characters, seemingly assembled for an exclusively Afro American reconstruction of 'Thriller.' Tom and Julian suddenly became fractious, the latter blurting, "'Ben, we're in the middle of 'CRACK CITY'...! Do you know where you're taking us or not...?"

"Calm down," I told him, "I know it's somewhere around here."

Despite the fleeting drama and fears of mutiny, we were less than 5 minutes walk from Bleecker Street and everybody's temper soon seemed a good deal better, drinking lager in the subterranean ambience of my new favourite bar. As the beer went down, Tom apologised for getting a little short with me.

We got talking to a long haired guy with a surf metal image who was evidently a regular and tended to give the impression that he had first refusal of the hottest alternative pussy. Julian thought he might be on coke. Any such inference was exciting to me since my chemical education was rather limited at this stage and I had yet to experience the dubious delights of the old 'marching powder.'

After a few more libations we departed in search of a place to eat. A diner that was advertising 'ALL THE BEER YOU CAN DRINK' with a certain menu option caught our collective eye. It looked like a challenge, or more likely a swindle thought Julian. He was half right. Perhaps they should have specified, 'All The Beer You Can Drink Provided You Can Prove You Are Over 21.' Julian was 22 but Tom and I were both 20 apiece and the restaurant proprietor wasn't having any of our excuses regarding the whereabouts of our passports.

Consequently, the waiter plied Julian with innumerable glasses of Coors Lite whilst Tom and I had to make to do with Diet Coke to wash down our victuals. I had been in New York for almost a week and this was my first experience of being refused an adult beverage. It would become more of an issue, the further west I travelled.

The next day I phoned my Uncle Lenny in Illinois. He sounded overjoyed to hear from me, exclaiming 'What are you doing in New York..?! Listen, you can stay here as long as you want to..."
Tom and Julian were bound for Colorado the next morning and I decided I would tag along to the station and catch a bus to Chicago. It looked like my best bet.

This being our last night in New York, I introduced the boys to Ray and Norman at the Greenwich Village apartment. Julian was convinced that Norman's girlfriend was a call girl and wouldn't be dissuaded from the idea. The fact that all 3 occupants were engaged in a game of scrabble when we arrived unannounced didn't seem to impact on his belief system.

We went for drinks and finished up in one of Ray's favourite haunts with salsa music and cocktails. Julian got talking to a light skinned black guy who was evidently a fine dancer and asked if he knew where he could get a joint. The dance floor king motioned to a friend and said, "Let's take a walk..." and the three of them exited the bar.

They were gone for over an hour, leading to ripples of concern in our ranks but duly returned around 1am, all smiles and transatlantic banter. Julian had enjoyed an impromptu sojourn of the surrounding neighbourhoods, in search of a morsel of marihuana after midnight. At one point he found it necessary to caution his new acquaintances, "If you boys have brought me all this way to skank me for 7 dollars then it really is a waste of your time..."

His charm and looks endeared him to everyone. In time I would dub him 'The Smarm King.'

14/ MY KIND OF TOWN (August 12 - to late September 1990)

"How can it cost twice as much to go half the fucking distance...?" I demanded to know against the backdrop of hustle and bustle at Port Authority Station on a Sunday afternoon. Julian and Tom had purchased Greyhound tickets to Denver, roughly 1800 miles from where we stood, for $79 each. Upon enquiry, I learned that the fare to Chicago, a mere 800 miles away, was $120. I was almost broke and resolutely unwilling to spend any more than I absolutely had to on the conveyance to my next destination, particularly if these two could get to Colorado for chump change.

I asked Julian if the Denver service stopped anywhere near Chicago. He approached a lady at one of the ticket kiosks and returned with the good news:

"It stops right in Chicago."

That was settled then. I would buy a ticket to Denver, get off in Chicago and save myself 40 bucks. The added bonus being that I could travel with friends. Things were looking up. At this precise moment I had no thoughts beyond getting to the Windy City as cheaply as possible but my frugality would have fateful repercussions down the line.

The journey took almost 19 hours and was a pretty wretched affair. It's fair to say that travel conditions were not enhanced by our rookie mistake of siting at the back of the coach in proximity of the toilet. Tom seemed to lose his sense of humour shortly after Cleveland but Julian remained good company.

Some of our fellow passengers would not have looked overtly out of place in a US prison biopic and the occasional argument broke out over one paltry thing or another. I once heard a person refer to the Greyhound bus service as 'the Black Person's Airline'. An odious analogy perhaps but not entirely without resonance.

The bus pulled into Chicago at just gone 9am on Monday, August 13. I bid the lads farewell and alluded to the possibility of meeting up again soon. Whenever, wherever, who knew...? I had to feel for them, having another day's travel ahead in such squalid conditions. I stepped off the coach with the unsteady gait of a person who has been confined to a sitting position for several hours and waited for my luggage to be retrieved from the hold. There were no dramas on this occasion.

Lenny had told me, "Don't talk to no black men or anything. Just catch the Rock Island District Line from Union Station to Midlothian. I'll be at work but I'll leave my house open."

The train ride from Chicago to Midlothian was perfectly straightforward but locating 14908 South Millard Avenue proved a little more challenging. It seemed implausible that so many domiciles could be located on what purported to be the same street as I wandered aimlessly through a maze of inoffensive bungalows with kempt lawns resembling every mid-western suburb I had seen in a hundred U.S sitcoms.

After about 20 minutes of fruitless ambulation, I stumbled upon a family sitting on their front porch and asked where I might find 14908 South Millard. After some initial problems understanding my accent, the lady of the house pointed me in the right direction.

Ten minutes later, I arrived outside Uncle Lenny's white detached residence, as the sprinkler system maintained the front lawn in his absence. The porch door was open as promised, so I entered the living room and threw my bag down on the creme sofa. There was a note from Lenny on the coffee table:

'HI BEN,

YOUR ROOM IS SECOND ON THE LEFT (THE ONE WITH THE WATERBED.) THE DOG IS CALLED BRANDY, SHE'S QUITE FRIENDLY. MY GIRLFRIEND, TERRI AND HER DAUGHTER, HEATHER, WILL COME AND SAY HELLO LATER.

I'LL BE BACK AROUND 7.

LENNY.'

Half an hour later, Terri and Heather showed up as promised to see how the visitor was settling in. Heather was 18, Ivy League hot and having sex with her seemed like an eminently agreeable idea. It turned out that she had a diminutive Mexican boyfriend of whom her absent father disapproved. Perhaps, aided by the devastating aphrodisiac properties of English charm, I might ingratiate myself. It was worth a shot.

Unfortunately, Heather could not be prised from the affections of her pint-sized Latin paramour and so I spent the next 6 weeks watching MTV, eating whatever Lenny brought home and necking endless American beers with my cousin Timmy and his friends. He was the same age as me but already had a 2 year old daughter although he still lived with his Mum in a house down the street from Lenny's

As we were both underage, Timmy would drive his truck to a predominantly black neighbourhood called Harvey in order to buy crates of beer from a liquor store where the management didn't ask questions. It seemed to be a very popular spot for white kids on that frustrating cusp of adulthood.

As stated, it was a predominantly black neighbourhood but, on my first weekend in Illinois, Heather's friend Jemma took me to a house party hosted by some white friends of theirs who happened to live in the area. The assembled guests made quite a fuss of me and my accent but I didn't stay for long. Upon hearing that I had yet to see Chicago proper, the elder brother of the host suggested we take a ride downtown.

Minutes later I was seated in the back of a white Chevrolet with my new best friend at the wheel and a guy who answered to the name of Kenny in the passenger seat. The driver, every inch my perception of a 'redneck' with shoulder length hair and a moustache, swigged beer from a red plastic cup with one hand on the steering wheel as we headed into the city at a pace that was probably at variance with state traffic laws.

"Like to get high, Ben...?" he asked, still slugging his beer.

"Sure.: What are you thinking...?", I replied.

"You do cocaine...?"

"I'll do it but I don't have coke money," I stressed.

"Don't worry about money, man," he assured me.

The drug search now taking priority, we swung by a local bar but 'the connection' evidently wasn't around. Back in the car, Scott suggested, "We could try the Gardens..?"

"Hey man...!", Kenny exclaimed, "This dude's not gonna' wanna' go to the GARDENS..."

Anxious not to seem like a hick, I stressed, "Go where we need to go, man. I'm cool..."

That settled it. We drove for about ten minutes before approaching a large expanse of waste ground. I couldn't see any evidence of a housing project in the background. Just barren land. As soon as we rolled up, the car was besieged by 20-30 young black males, all advertising their alleged narcotic wares in a cacophony of urban entrepreneurial spirit.

"I GOT COKE

I GOT WEED,.."

"WHADDYA' NEED...?"

It was unlike anything I'd ever seen before and if I'd been remotely street savvy, I'd certainly have told the pair of them what a monumentally silly venture it was. It happened very quickly. Engulfed by a teeming mass of dark faces, Scott asked for cocaine in whatever weighed denomination was normal in these parts.

He proffered 60 dollars out of the window in exchange for a transparent packet of white powder. The kid who took the money looked about 12 but it was hard to be chronologically precise as he and his confederates sped off into the night, as quickly as they had appeared.

Scott opened the packet and tasted a dab with his tongue. Disgusted, he growled, "It's soap...!"

Apparently the eternal optimist, Kenny reasoned that perhaps it had been cut with something.

"Kenny, it's SOAP, man...! I got a crowbar in the trunk.. I oughta' go back there and kick me some nigger asses...!"

"C'mon, we'll get shot, man. Let's get outta' here."

I figured Scott was whistling in the dark. He didn't strike me as a gargantuan intellectual but I doubted he was stupid enough to commit suicide on this notorious patch of waste ground.

"Let's go...", I concurred. Scott knew it made sense and put the Chevy into gear.

Now it was about damage limitation. Scott drove back to the first bar we had visited and left me and Kenny in the car while he went inside to look for his regular contact. He returned minutes later with a tiny amount of what was supposedly cocaine and split it three ways as we each snorted a threadbare line off the dashboard through a rolled up ten dollar bill.

Scott was now in sufficiently high spirits to continue our expedition downtown but I was rather disappointed, having heard so much about the mythical effects of Colombia's most famous export. Either I hadn't had enough or we'd been ripped off again, I figured. But it wasn't the end of the world and not as if I had paid for any of it, soap powder included.

Playing the tour guide, Scott pointed out Soldier's Field, home of the Chicago Bears, as we neared our destination. Inevitably, I was compelled to tell him that the famous football stadium had also been the site of Dempsey - Tunney 2, the legendary 'Battle of the Long Count.' They liked this glam rock boy with the 'regal' accent who talked about fighting and was up for a line of bad coke.

"I like the way this dude thinks," Scott affirmed. "That's the only reason I'm taking him downtown."

Our chauffeur cruised around, delineating various of Chicago's notable tourist attractions, for about half an hour but we never actually got out of the car. His obligation to show me the lights fulfilled, we were soon on the expressway heading back to Harvey and the house Scott shared with his parents and younger brother, Billy. It was after 1am when we arrived and the keg party was over, with no sign of life inside.

Presumably not wishing to wake his folks, he ushered us into the garage at the front of the house where he had some beers and a quarter bottle of Jack Daniels. As we sat in straight back chairs drinking from cans and taking turns with the JD, Kenny spoke of the time he went to a strip bar in Toronto where they have 'no rules against nudity.'

"I could smell this bitch's snatch, man...!" he claimed.

I was keen to uncover the Rock N' Roll dream but it wasn't falling into place just yet. We finished the alcohol before Kenny made his excuses and headed home. At this point, it was too late for me to get back to Lenny's so I slept on the living room couch at Scott's invitation. Heather and Jemma came to pick me up in the morning and joked that Scott was a bad influence on their new English friend.

A couple of weeks later, I got to try some real cocaine at the house of one of Timmy's friends. Matt was evidently a small time drug dealer but his parents, with whom he lived, seemed to know nothing about it. Regardless, we clubbed together and purchased what Timmy referred to as 'half a T' one Friday night and, suddenly, I could see what all the fuss was about.

After snorting a couple of lines, I felt full of wisdom and exuberance, as one does. Before too long, I was waxing lyrical in a manner that made a few of Timmy's redneck mates a tad uncomfortable. My contempt for patriotism and the American flag plus how I wanted to have sex with a black girl before I left this mortal coil. Vaguely alarmed and embarrassed in equal measure, my cousin saw fit to explain, "He's cool, guys, he's just from a totally different background."

It was 6am when I got back to the house. Lenny was getting ready for work, so I sat at the breakfast table talking at him with an enthusiasm that probably wasn't entirely normal for early morning protocol He nodded politely. He was a man of the world and probably suspected that I was chemically fuelled in some way or other.

At any rate, I felt as if my welcome mat at 14908 South Millard Avenue was wearing thin. I had enjoyed Lenny's hospitality for 6 weeks now and needed to make a decision regarding the next move. It was late September and I had next to no money left. I had been away for a respectable amount of time. Long enough to avoid derisory censure from Andy and the old man if I chose to return home without future ado.

But, in my heart, I was well aware that, besides a week in New York and an ill advised detour to a ghetto drug hot spot, I had basically stayed in sleepy suburbia for 6 weeks, being fed by my Uncle throughout. This was hardly the epiphanic rite of passage that the trip was supposed to represent.

In actual fact, I didn't have enough cash to cover my fare back to Newark in order to fly home to London, even if I'd wanted to. What I did have was a Greyhound ticket to Denver, purchased several weeks ago for reasons of economy, already explained. Perhaps I could still use it to catch a bus out West...?

As always, it was worth a try.

15/ THINGS TO DO IN DENVER WHEN YOU'RE DEADBEAT (Late September 1990)

I called the number on the back of my ticket to enquire if it was still valid for Denver, despite having broken my journey in Chicago several weeks ago. A female voice confirmed, "Yes, sir. All tickets are valid within 3 months of the date of purchase to the named destination." What a fantastic policy. Ironically, the Greyhound might have been slow but it was ludicrously cheap and user friendly.

I swung by Timmy's Mum's house to say my goodbyes and bought a bunch of flowers for Terri plus a bottle of vodka for Lenny by way of token thanks. My trusty blue holdall, already more well travelled than its owner, was packed and ready for the next chapter.

That evening, Heather gave me a lift to Union Station which was awfully decent of her. I never did get to meet the swarthy midget who was banging her but consoled myself with the notion that she would live to regret the dormancy of my unrequited lust when I was a Rock Star. As she pulled up near the station, I bid her farewell with a chaste peck on the cheek before getting out of the car and retrieving my bag from the trunk

Having located the outbound Denver service, I flashed my crumpled ticket at the driver and sat at the back of the coach next to a couple of English lads who had been working as Rickshaw drivers on the Atlantic City

Boardwalk. Also seated in our proximity was a feisty young Puerto Rican chick with a young child who freely informed various of her fellow commuters that she was running away from an abusive partner. This was going to be an even longer haul than the New York to Chicago trek so I was grateful tor a bit of colour.

The journey took 22 hours and, aside from snatching a bit of broken sleep, I spent most of it talking to my two young compatriots. One was ginger and bespectacled whilst the other had prematurely thinning hair. For me, hair loss was roughly akin to leprosy and I almost feared that it might be contagious. It just seemed so tragic to be struck down in one's prime with an ailing thatch where there should be a tousled androgynous glory. Retrospectively, I blame the media and my mother for this enduring hang up.

Aesthetic judgements aside, I was most interested in their immigration status in the USA. I knew it was imperative that I find a job as soon as I arrived in Denver but wasn't sure how easy it was going to be. Seeking encouragement, I asked it the rickshaw gig had been a cash in hand affair but it turned out they both had working visas and social security numbers. The ginger guy showed me his SS card and I made a mental note of the formation of letters and numbers, already scheming that I might need some bogus digits to aid my quest for gainful employment. It proved to be a good move.

Being the organised types, my friends also had a Denver guidebook. I perused the accommodation section and found a youth hostel in the Capitol Hill district that only charged $6 a night. I would stay there, I decided. No more Vanderbilt extravagance for me. Evidently, I was learning on the road.

The bus rolled into Denver Station at 7pm on a Wednesday evening. The two English lads decided they would pitch in with me at the hostel in Capitol Hill. "Can't go wrong for 6 dollars," said the ginger guy. They wanted to get a cab but I argued that it didn't make sense to find a dirt cheap accommodation and shell out for a taxi. My reasoning was upheld and so we caught a tram to our mutual destination, 2 miles from the City Centre.

The hostel was a charming little place with a benign regime and a Mancunian girl on reception who'd have passed for a goth. She explained that the management kept the price so attractively low on the understanding that we guests performed a token chore every morning, be it washing up or cleaning. It sounded like a drag but one could hardly be disgruntled for half the price of a round of drinks. Unlike the Vanderbilt, all the rooms were 8 bed dormitories. Privacy was a commodity and it cost more than 6 bucks a night.

I spent most of the next day getting a feel for the city which, in terms of commerce and tourism, seemed to revolve around the 16th Street Mall. Compared to New York, Denver seemed like a Village but that wasn't necessarily a bad thing, I concluded. The hostel had an agreeable mix of Europeans, Americans, Asians and the odd Latino backpacker. This was what I came for. Bright young things from all corners of the globe on their various quests for adventure and self knowledge. It was all starting to make sense.

By Friday morning, coincidentally or not, I was down to my last 6 dollars. The previous day, I had seen an advert in the local paper that proclaimed:

INSTANT MUSCLE REQUIRED
 Want Work...? We've Got it

Start Today, Work On The Days To Suit You.

The Stand By Agency
2870 Bryant Street
Denver,
CO 80211

It looked promising with no mention of unwanted bureaucracy. I decided to take a trip to the given address, accompanied by another English guy who was looking for diversion on his last day in Denver, having been in town to see Bob Dylan the night before.

The office was located in an industrial area about 30 minutes' walk from the city centre. As I sat in line and waited for my number to be called, the first discouraging omen was a sign on the wall:

'WE DO NOT EMPLOY ILLEGAL ALIENS

YOU WILL NEED TO SHOW PROOF OF
YOUR AUTHORISATION TO WORK IN THE USA
UPON REGISTRATION.'

I filled out the cursory application form, leaving the visa section blank, whilst waiting to be summoned to the next available counter. I had a plan. Admittedly, it was a long shot but, being 5000 miles from home and on the verge of destitution, I had absolutely nothing to lose. Even the worst case scenario would presumably result in swift repatriation and I was guessing it wouldn't cost me a dime.

When the time came, I motioned for my confederate to follow me to the window. There was something about his honest to goodness British Backpacker appearance that seemed to lead credence to my imminent ruse. I liked to think that I looked dangerously subversive.

The gentleman behind the counter, a dark haired bespectacled guy in his early 30s, clearly shared the almost compulsory affection that Americans seem to have for their English cousins. I had a good feeling about him.

"You guys working your way around the States...?" he cheerfully enquired.

"Yes," I concurred. "My friend here is leaving today but I feel like staying a little longer."

"You like Colorado...?"

"Love it," I assured him.

I was ready to roll the dice. I held up my application form before saying, "I have a potential problem. One of my bags got stolen in New York and my Social Security card was in it…. I'm still waiting on a replacement."

"Do you have your passport, buddy…?"

"Yes."

"Do you know your social security number..?"

"I do, as it happens, mate."

"Ok Ben. Write your social security in the box right here, I'll go have a word with my supervisor."

I took the pen and scrawled the digits I had memorised based on the authentic lines of the ginger guy's social security number before passing the form back under the counter. At that moment, an older man with a passing resemblance to Kenny Rogers appeared.

"Bill, his wallet got stolen in New York… He has a social security number but is still waiting for a new card. What can we do here…?"

Bill seemed bored, "If he has a valid foreign passport and his visa hasn't expired then he's good to go. Sign him up…!"

The dark haired guy took a photocopy of my passport and returned minutes later with an orange badge bearing my name, the Stand By Agency logo and the fictitious social security number I had just given him.

"Ok, Ben. You're all good. This is all you need to show when you come in for work here."

I could scarcely believe it had been so easy. I didn't spare a thought for what was going to happen when the relevant agency attempted to deduct tax from the bogus identity that had just been created. So far as I was concerned, I had shown a willingness to pay a kick back to Uncle Sam and my conscience was clear.

To compound my good fortune, a labouring job had just come in and the dark haired guy said it could use another pair of hands if I wanted to start right away. Nodding affirmatively, I was hastily introduced to a pair of Mexicans who had also been waiting in line, one of whom had a car to transport us to the site.

I worked from 1pm to 7pm, moving office furniture and clearing rubble at a business premises on the outskirts of Denver. My co-workers were mostly Hispanic and seemed like a friendly bunch. I told one of the guys that I was working my way to Los Angeles. He smiled, "When I first came to this country, I was exactly the same..."

I felt rather pleased with myself. 5000 light years from home, on the edge of bankruptcy, I suddenly had the power to sustain my American Dream. A job was something I had never previously regarded as a commodity. Now I had several jobs, dependent on the more urgent requirements for unskilled labour in the Denver catchment area.

At the end of the shift, the supervisor signed off our tickets before I bundled back into the car with the Mexicans. They told me that the office didn't shut until 8pm and so there was still time to swing by and pick up our wages. It really had been a good day.

20 minutes later, the 3 of us stood in line, awaiting our remuneration for the afternoon's toil. I presented my ticket at the counter and a lady gave me 22 dollars and 80 cents. 6 hours at $3.80 an hour, or minimum wage. It might not seem a great deal but to me it was like a fortune from the sky.

I went back to the hostel to freshen up and decided it was time to give Julian a call. Using a payphone on the street, I called the number he had given me for Mario and heard his affluent English timbre in perfect contrast to the U.S dial tone.

"What's happening...? I'm in Denver..."

"Ben, mate...! Me and the rest of the band are meeting up at the guitarist's place in Denver tonight for a bit of a drink. Do you want to come over...?"

"Yeah, alright, where is it, mate...?"

"It's on the 16th Street Mall, above Ivory's Piano Bar. If you come at 9, press the top bell and ask for Ted. But we'll all be there...."

16/ THE BOYS IN THE BAND

I waked from Capitol Hill and found 'Ivory's at the near end of 16th street. After pressing the top bell, somebody buzzed me in before Julian came bounding out of the lift holding a red plastic cup of weak American beer.

'How's it fucking going mate...? You survived Chicago...!"

"Of course...!" I retorted.

We stepped in the lift and ascended to an open plan loft style apartment. Our host, every inch the California Rock guitarist stereotype with longish blonde hair, T- Shirt and shorts, extended his hand. "What's up...? I'm Ted."

The as yet unnamed band was a 5 piece. Mario, Hispanic in appearance and stocky of build was the unofficial leader. Adam, the keyboard player was olive skinned and a tad aloof. Before long he would become the whipping boy. Keith, the bass player, was the token intellectual. Unmistakably Anglo Saxon, bespectacled with high temples and facial hair that made him look older than his 20 years. It quickly became apparent that he didn't drink alcohol. I couldn't understand why anyone would choose not to drink, unless they happened to be an elite athlete. Especially not a person who was in a rock band.

Keith's abstinence notwithstanding, the beer flowed. And so did the J germeister which was clearly the exotic tipple of choice in this particular gang. Ted had a girlfriend called Susan. Blonde and trophy hot but also terribly nice and not the least bit 'up herself.' Allegedly, she was Canadian.

After roughly an hour of civilised beverages and a breaking of the ice, the band launched into an impromptu rehearsal with everyone taking their relevant positions in the expansive living space. The first number they played was 'Dancing In The Moonlight'. They sounded good, if a little inoffensive for my tastes. Julian sang and played guitar way better than I did and so I naturally felt a little envious.

They didn't know too many songs together at this early stage and so the rehearsal soon descended into a jam. Thereafter, everyone besides Keith drank beer and intermittent shots of 'Jag' before passing out pretty much where they fell.

The next morning, they joked about their innocuous hangovers as a pact was made to go to a nearby diner in search of breakfast. Susan was apparently at work and so it was a boys only affair. As soon as we were seated in a bustling restaurant of Ted's recommendation he lamented, "She didn't even kiss me goodbye when she left..." before turning to me and asking "Did she kiss YOU goodbye....?"

It was decreed that the band liked me and so Ted suggested it would be cool to have a roadie on board. Mario agreed and calculated that such a service would be worth 25 bucks a night as the others nodded in approbation. It sounded good to me. More crucially, Keith said I was welcome to share his dorm on Campus in Boulder. Economically, he was the least well situated of the group but it's often those who have the least that tend to give the most.

After breakfast, Julian approached the waitress he regarded as the prettiest and asked if she would like to join us for drinks that evening at the apartment. His sense of God given entitlement with the ladies was almost an affront to my threadbare 'game' but she politely declined, nonetheless.

That night, there was more drinking and shenanigans. The upshot was Mario being left naked in the downstairs reception area whilst Ted frantically took pictures with a hastily sourced camera. High jinks indeed. The snaps were developed the next morning and Mario took it all in good spirits despite seeming livid and morose in equal measure the night before.

This temporary emotional slump was blamed on a Native American Indian that he and Julian had bumped into earlier in the evening whilst out for beers. As the man approached them for change, Mario apparently felt inordinately sorry for this browbeaten figure who had been 'raped' by colonialism. He proceeded to cry whilst proffering whatever cash he had in his pockets. Allegedly, having found a sympathetic ear, the man had introduced himself as 'Way Waywardson'

Over Sunday lunch in a Mexican flavoured restaurant, I suggested they should call the band 'Way Waywardson' in homage to this incident. On the spur of the moment, my idea was supported although it was a lousy name on reflection. Keith made his excuses and left early after giving me a piece of paper on which he had written his address. It was arranged that I would make my way over that evening to take immediate advantage of his generous offer.

After hanging at Ted's for a few more hours watching TV, I caught a bus to Boulder. Keith lived in a block of dorms located at the top of College Avenue, near the epicentre of student night life in the beautiful Rocky Mountain town. He was in his second year at the University of Colorado, although I never did ask what he was studying. The room was very small, containing a single bed, a wooden desk and chair with communal kitchen and bathroom facilities on the other side of the corridor. I would be sleeping on the floor.

"Forgive me but I can't offer you a meal" he explained as I sat down at the desk, "I'm on a very tight budget."

There was no denying that his circumstances were almost unbearably frugal. Keith lived on ramen noodles and Kool Aid. He had just enough to survive the Fall semester and philanthropy was not an option. I was grateful for the offer of a place to rest my head but something would clearly have to be done about the catering.

Food rationing aside, it was clear that Keith and I had much in common. He might have been 'straight edge' but we were both angry young men. Deep thinkers who loved music and despised mediocrity and injustice in all forms. We talked about all of those things and more before we fell asleep.

17/ ACID (October 1990)

The next night I went out for drinks with Julian to see what Boulder had to offer a couple of sex hungry English musicians. When it came to the musician tag, I was heavily riding his coattails but, as the token roadie, I was in the band so far as I was concerned. We ended up in a hip student bar/restaurant called 'The Sink' which had murals on the walls. The most prominent illustration - 'in honour of our star janitor, Robert Redford. After cleaning up at The Sink he went on to clean up in Hollywood.'

Near closing time we got talking to an attractive young lady who gave her name as Shannon. She was visibly inebriated and seemingly available. Julian made the early running before she announced, "You guys are so cute...! You can both sleep in my bed tonight... It's ok.. I've had a threesome before..."

I'd been told that American girls were forward and this seemed like a wonderful confirmation but Julian balked. Taking me to one side he said, "Either you fuck her or I fuck her tonight. I'm not into seeing your arse pumping away..." The Smarm King simply had too many options to entertain such debauchery. As it happened, Shannon's virtue would remain perfectly intact on this occasion albeit by accident rather than design.

As last orders were called she insisted we bundle into a car with her group of friends. Unfortunately, the cold night air induced its familiar nausea on the drunken and she threw up over her shoes before being jostled into the backseat. Amorous thoughts now banished; it was all about whether Shannon could remember where she lived. The designated driver didn't seem too sure. By process of elimination, we eventually found the place she called home and everyone bar the driver got out of the vehicle. As a less drunk female friend walked her carefully to the door it was perfectly apparent that nobody would be getting so much as a peck on the cheek.

Empty handed, Julian and I walked back to Mario's house which, mercifully, wasn't too far away from the suburb we had found ourselves in. I would have to crash on the couch. Before nodding off, I consoled myself that there would be other promiscuous American chicks who could handle their drink.

Boulder reminded me of Stroud but with 50 times the potential for adventure, both carnal and narcotic. Culturally, it was a throwback to 1967 with copious swathes of tie dye and posters of Jim Morrison, The Grateful Dead, The Beatles and The Stones. Despite its limited land mass, the town was host to some 25, 000 students. I calculated that at least 8, 000 of those were nubile young women.

There were keg parties almost every night which allowed me to get drunk for nothing and the girls really did go crazy for an English accent. Consequently, my trips to Denver to pick up bits of work at the Stand By Agency became more sporadic. So long as I could lay my hands on something to eat every day, drinking and socialising wasn't a problem.

At one particular party, I was decidedly pissed when I asked some dark haired vixen for her phone number. Julian was a card carrying pick up artist and always seemed to ask for digits early so I followed his lead. I ended up with an impressive collection of phone numbers but little else. I enjoyed the attention and appearance of popularity but couldn't seem to close the deal.

In this instance, neither of us could find pen or paper and so she scrawled the number on my forearm with mascara. The next thing I knew, Julian and I were in a taxi, en route to another shindig at a large house on the outskirts of town. As soon as we arrived, someone seemed to mention LSD at which I blurted, "Can you get us some...?"

Julian took control of the situation, evidently purchasing 2 pieces of blotter paper before handing one to me and warning, "Ben, take HALF...." Deaf to such counsel, I swallowed the whole thing on the spot before wandering into the kitchen where I bumped into Ted. Surprised to see him, I announced, "Hey Ted.. I'm on acid...." Perhaps he heard, 'I want acid' as he handed me another tab from his pocket which I also guzzled immediately.

2 hits for my first psychedelic experiment, paralytic drunk, 4,500 miles from home. What could possibly go wrong...?

There was a perfect blank of unknown duration and then I was fighting on a slippery green lawn against many assailants. There was noise, panic, voices and the crashing of knuckles on bone. One of my adversaries was brandishing something silver. It was mesmerising and beautiful. Somebody said it was a knife. Then I heard Julian...

"LEAVE HIM ALONE... ! CAN'T YOU SEE HE'S TRIPPING OUT OF HIS HEAD....?"

At this point, an older gentleman of around 40 intervened, putting his arm around me and saying, "It's ok, Ben... BREATHE...." The melee was dispersed as Julian and my new friend walked me to a more secluded area of the garden where we sat down on deckchairs. The older guy was called John and he seemed to know a thing or two about LSD.

He told me to expunge myself of negative or aggressive thoughts. Observe. Breathe. Relax. I suddenly had an overwhelming sense of detached wisdom and serenity. 'Father forgive them for they know not what they do....' But, still, I was confused.

"What does it all mean...?", I asked.

"Ben, if we define it, we limit it... But aren't we lucky to have this...?" John replied before apparently disappearing.

Seemingly in an instant, the sun came up over Boulder and the scene was of discarded cans and bottles, a few stragglers asleep on couches behind the patio doors. Still utterly twisted, we made our excuses and left, Julian at pains to apologise to a sawn off young sorority type for my swashbuckling behaviour. I assumed she must have lived in the house.

We walked for what might have been a thousand miles before we came to an empty baseball arena, presumably connected to the CU. Julian said it was too early to go back to Mario's so we sat in the stands and attempted to have a conversation. Nothing made sense and everything was comical. I thought I could hear children chanting in unison. But I couldn't make out what they were saying.

We walked some more and eventually arrived at Mario's house. Mario and Debbie were out. Perhaps Julian has been waiting for them to vacate before daring to enter in our drug addled state. "Something to drink perhaps...?" I suggested. He went to the kitchen and made me a glass of orange cordial before I proclaimed, "LOOK at my arm...! Can you see numbers...?

"Yeah..' he shrugged.

"Perhaps it's some kind of code...?"

"It's that chick from last night's number... She wrote it on your arm. Don't you remember...?"

Disastrously, I decided to call the number from Mario's landline. Unsurprisingly, a young American girl answered but she didn't sound like the one I had met about 14 hours earlier. I didn't know who I was asking for which obviously didn't help.

"Heather....did you meet a foreign guy last night...?"

It turns out Heather did. She comes to the phone sounding impatient. She was 'watching a movie...' I'm pretty sure it was the worst attempted phone seduction in history. The facility of texting must have revolutionised a generation of sex lives but I was born too soon. After an awkward 3 minutes of miscommunication, I hung up as Julian collapsed on the floor in a paroxysm of hysterical laughter.

The remainder of the day passed quickly and before long in was back in Keith's tiny room, relating my misadventure. I was tired, drained and clearly had a lot to learn.

18/ CHEQUE MATE (November 1990)

Desperate times called for desperate measures. Being a thoroughly decent chap, Keith had relented on his no sharing policy but I couldn't stomach much more Cherry Kool Aid or wretched noodles, regardless. It was Sunday evening, I was hungry as hell and about ready to slay a distant relative in exchange for a couple of beers. But I had an idea.

"Maybe they will accept one of my cheques at The Sink...? If they do, we can eat like Kings and I can get a drink."

Alcohol was no incentive for Keith but he was as hungry as I was and had to be even wearier of dehydrated wheat. He considered it worth a try and so we donned our coats and headed down College Avenue. Knowing that my cheque book was full of meaningless promissory notes in pound sterling for an account that was already overdrawn, I briefly pondered the moral aspect.

"Morals come with money, Ben," Keith insisted as we quickened our step in the cold November night. Arriving at our destination, we chose a table and a beauteous girl by the name of Sarah came to take our order.

"Excuse me, Miss, but can you accept an English cheque...?"

Sarah had no idea but went off in search of a man who did. The young manager clearly had no expertise in international banking affairs but the collective national faith in a British accent won the day as he shrugged and said, "Go ahead...."

Bingo. I ordered the king size burger with hickory sauce and fries plus a large pitcher of beer. Keith ordered a tuna melt. Sarah departed and we sat across the table beaming at one another. The high life beckoned and it was hard to conceal the mutual sense of triumph.

The moment was savoured for as long as it reasonably could be. Long enough for me to drink 2 pitchers of beer and feel that familiar warm glow of optimism and invincibility. Both qualities would come in handy as I prepared to sign the spurious cheque. Backed as it was by the spurious piece of plastic from Barclays Bank bearing the caption, 'THIS IS NOT A CHEQUE GUARANTEE CARD.'

Absurdly and with absolute confidence, I asked lovely Sarah, "Shall I just cross out the pound sign and change it to a dollar...?"

"Yeah, I guess that would be the thing to do..."

"Can I include your tip...?"

"Oh thank you, Sir...!"

I made out the cheque for ten dollars more than the price of the meal. Travel is about self discovery and I was a big tipper, it transpired. Sarah smiled and said, "Please come again...!"

Thereafter, we rinsed the joint, lunch and dinner, for a fortnight. It was called 'The Sink' after all. We always asked for Sarah, who seemed perpetually at work, and always gave her a fat tip. No sense in explaining the vagaries of currency conversion to another wide eyed young bint if we could avoid it.

Sometimes we brought guests in order to share our newfound opulence, including Mario on one occasion who seemed a little nervous throughout. Perhaps he had a hard time believing that anyone was gullible enough to accept this continual flow of worthless paper in exchange for food and beer. Then one midweek afternoon, the game was up.

As we entered the premises, Sarah intercepted us near the door, saying, "Guys, I'm really sorry but we can't accept those cheques anymore. The bank sent them back. You're more than welcome to dine here but we must ask for an alternative method of payment."

Having quickly established that we were not under arrest and nobody appeared to be demanding recompense, we made token apology and exited forthwith. In an abject display of gall we then walked straight into Taylor's, not 50 yards up the street, attempting to pull off the same coup. Astonishingly, it worked. I even had the cheek to inform the manager that I had used my trusty cheques at The Sink and there hadn't been a problem. And so we ate hamburgers with guacamole, our pleasure accentuated by the panoramic views that the roof garden afforded.

Taylor's was the hip place to play for up and coming campus bands and it was there that Way Warywardson played their maiden gig. On the night I invited a cute little blonde chick called Adie, whom I'd met at a party the week before. I told her I was in the band although the ruse would be hard to maintain when she noted my conspicuous absence on the small stage. Actually, I did have a cameo in the set, singing the Ramones classic 'I Wanna Be Sedated.' It was Mario's idea and gave me that little bit of credibility. Julian was too AOR to pull off a punk ditty like that.

As a roadie, I proved more detrimental than helpful, somehow managing to damage one of Ted's prized possessions during a simple string change. But I got my 25 dollars all the same. Singing in front of live audiences and hanging around for numerous hours of rehearsals, I was becoming a passable guitarist. I was also learning to drink with a vengeance. And why not...? Julian drank a lot and it didn't seem to do him any harm.

At some point, Chris paid us a visit. He was in the States on business and had a few days to kill, so the 3 of us holed up in a motel at his expense. Upon arrival, he could see the metamorphosis and didn't much care for it. From the vaguely reserved teen who seldom got drunk to this reinvented beer monster who spoke of 'chicks and tarts' and Class A narcotics. "I shouldn't have put you two together,' he said.

On the second night of his stay, we had a drunken argument in a bar. A very camp gay black guy was chatting me up and the incident proved to be a catalyst for discord. Chris said that I treated women purely as sex objects and so why should I have an issue with being objectified...? "So he wants to shove 10 inches of black dick up your arse... Big deal...!" he added for good measure.

I was far too insecure not to bite and so I blasted back, implying that a lonely old rich faggot of his ilk was good for nothing but bar tabs.

"Get laid and then come and talk to me," he suggested.

I was enraged at this blatant puncturing of my carefully crafted facade. Here I was, masquerading as a bon vivant lothario when I hadn't actually got to first base with an American girl. He was raining on my parade and my reaction was to sulk profusely. Consequently, I didn't speak to Chris for the next 48 hours, although I wasn't proud enough to spurn his hospitality. Due to the bad atmosphere, he elected to visit relatives in North Carolina but still paid for Julian and I to spend a few more nights in the motel.

Stubbornly, I refused to say goodbye when he left for the airport for which Julian scolded me. It turned out that Chris had given him a hundred dollars to pass on to me before he left. It should have made me feel bad but it didn't. I wouldn't speak to Chris for another 6 years.

19/ MY BIG FAT GREEK AFFRAY (December 1990)

After those few more nights at the motel, I was back to slumming it with Keith. Having struck out at The Sink and not wanting to push things at Taylor's, we needed a revenue stream to feed our new expectations. One night we sold fake drugs at a Frat Party although it wasn't entirely premeditated.

Across the street lived a quartet of student kids with whom I used to socialise. One of them had family in England and a bizarre hybrid accent. His name was Richard or Rich to his friends. He came by one afternoon and asked where I had been for the last few days. Naturally, I told him that Keith and I had been on a cocaine run to Taos, New Mexico. It was intended purely as an innocent wind up but ramifications followed.

A couple of nights later, inspired by boredom, Keith and I poured detergent and salt into a transparent plastic bag and claimed it was our freshly acquired 'stash.' Playing good cop/ bad cop, I permitted Rich a token sample while Keith protested, in keeping with his square image. He snorted a line and seemed to think he was 'buzzin'.

If Rich's mesolimbic pathway could be so easily manipulated then perhaps there was commercial potential in all of this. The following night, the 3 of us went to a house party and put it about that we were 'holding.' We sold our wares at $30 per half gram, although we obviously hadn't bothered to weigh the little parcels of nonsense that were suddenly flying out like hot cakes.

A little later, when I became properly absorbed into the UK drug scene, it would have been morally reprehensible. I learned that you didn't rip people off. It was dangerous and taboo. But, in my naivety so far from home, it didn't seem like anything besides a big wheeze to get one over on a handful of frat boy jocks.

Money changed hands and people went to the bathroom in binary pacts. I wasn't afraid of any physical retribution but neither did it seem clever to hang around and give anyone the time to realise they had been scammed. So we took the money and ran. Keith went home to bed but I sought refuge at a small gathering in another random student apartment where some long hair swapped me 7 tabs of acid in exchange for 'a line.'

This guy was drug savvy and knew it was pure bullshit on first taste. "Dude, you can keep the acid but that's NOT coke...." It seemed a good time to leave.

Back at home base, I plotted up in the communal kitchen so as not to wake Keith and swallowed all 7 tabs in increments of 2, 2 and 3. It was a ludicrous thing to do and proved I had learned nothing from the previous debacle. The ensuing 40 hours were fairly horrific. I couldn't sleep and at no point did I really find myself in a good space.

I watched the tiny black and white TV for several hours and allowed the acid to marinate in my cerebral cortex. Elvis Presley was singing some non-vegan friendly number about chicken fricassee. At daybreak, I went for a walk and ran into a student of my acquaintances by the name of Brad Bender. He was something of a geek but the hippychicks seemed to like him. Today, he was standing under a tree, gazing at a pair of converse sneakers that had been tied to an unreachably high branch by whatever means.

"Dude, I really wanna' get those shoes. I need like a knife on a big stick...."

I was feeling very fragile and he wasn't helping. I had to get away. I walked in the opposite direction and saw Rich sitting outside a cheap Mexican bistro with his friend, Axel. He seemed to have cooled on me since the shenanigans of the night before and offered no more than a cursory greeting. As I walked away, I was convinced I could hear him talking about what a thoroughly bad cove I was.

That night in the kitchen, I watched Mike Tyson annihilate Alex Stewart on HBO. Before the fight, they aired a short documentary by Spike Lee in which Don King shrieked, "I love white people. I love them like they love ME...." How profound, I thought. Spike's film lasted a lot longer than Stewart.

I had dropped the acid on a Friday night. By early Sunday evening, I was on the verge of losing my increasingly tenuous grip on reality. Too many malevolent forces seemed to surround me. Then a higher voice kicked in. I suddenly saw myself analogous to a car on a busy motorway. Certain death if the driver lost control and veered left or right but no drama if he could simply stay in lane and keep his foot on the gas. 'CONTROL YOUR VEHICLE' said the voice.

At that moment, I could hear 'Strawberry Fields Forever' playing in a nearby room.

'Living is easy with eyes closed.
Misunderstanding all you see
It's getting hard to be someone but it all works out
It doesn't matter much to me..'

It was time to sleep but I was going to be ok

The last gig Way Waywardson ever played was at the Sig Ep Fraternity House just before the Christmas Break. It was a ragged affair that saw Mario get so mortally drunk he had to be replaced by a random chick from the crowd who turned out to be a pretty good drummer. Earlier in the week, Adam had announced he was quitting the band which had created a bad vibe. Whilst nobody liked him anyway, his departure was still seen as a betrayal.

Minutes after the second set concluded, I punched a heavy set Jock type who had allegedly called me a faggot and all hell broke loose. As a pitched battle ensued, Keith and Julian bundled me out of the house, believing my presence to be the most incendiary. They told me to get off home and forget about packing up the gear. I pretended to acquiesce before striding back into the melee, only to be met with a hail of drum sticks thrown by Mario who was screaming, "BEN... GET OUT OF HERE..! YOU'LL GET KILLED..."

Knowing I was far from sober, Keith put a hand on my shoulder and said, "Ben... I want you to LISTEN to me because I'm your FRIEND. You have proved your point and now you need to leave. Take the keys and please GO..."

The calmness of his voice circumvented my ego and I did as he asked.

When we congregated the next day for the inevitable 'post-mortem' Mario said I should still get my 25 dollars because I had 'defended the band's honour.'

"I wish I'd seen you fuck that guy up, though.." he admitted wistfully.

It wasn't the most joyous of farewell scenes. Keith was packed and ready to fly back to Massachusetts for Christmas. Call it irony but my plans were a little more up in the air. While not elated with the situation, he was too solid of a guy to put me out on the street in his absence. As always, my exit strategy was a castle built on sand but it just might work.

If it didn't then I had little to look forward to over the festive period besides isolation and the 2 packets of Ramen Noodles that languished on the shelf. The student population had evacuated in its entirety, transforming Boulder into a ghost town, and Julian had left over a week ago. The party was over. Hawking his suitcase and guitar out of the door, he shrugged, "Well, good luck... Stay in touch."

"You too, mate. Be lucky..."

It was December 22 and I still had no money to get back to Newark in order to catch a flight home. Fortuitously, a few days earlier I had seen an airline ticket for sale on a student notice board, flying from Denver to Newark. The seller had promised to hold it for me and tonight was the deadline for me to come up with the cash. Since I had no cash, I called to ask if he would take a cheque. Barely able to conceal his disgust he replied, "Well, I've got no choice now...."

Indeed he didn't. It would have been hard enough finding a student left on Campus at this point, never mind one who required an urgent conveyance to New Jersey. It wasn't 'cricket' on my part but it was an offer he couldn't refuse, all the same. We arranged to meet early evening to make good the exchange.

When I arrived at his room in a similar block of dorms to the one Keith stayed in, he grudgingly handed over the ticket and asked for my passport or driving license number as collateral security. I told him that I had neither.

"Look, mate. I'm really sorry about this. I didn't intend to put you in this position but these are unforeseen circumstances. I'll give you my Dad's address and phone number...."

I asked for a pen and wrote the details on the back of the worthless cheque. I gave the real address and the real number. I didn't want to rip this guy off, I just couldn't pay him until I got back on English soil. He wasn't best pleased but the futility of his position has already been outlined. I saw myself out.

He must have thought I was lying about not having a passport but I wasn't. I didn't need one for the internal flight and, thereafter, I would be attempting to get from Newark to Gatwick without the most basic legal requirement. An explanation might be in order:

For the first few weeks in Boulder, I had been getting into bars using an old ID card of Ted's. I bore a very fleeting resemblance to the picture so it worked until the night I was refused entry to a Johnny Winter gig at Boulder Theatre and the bouncer confiscated the ID. A contingency was needed but since we are talking about a serious criminal offence, I shall be deliberately vague.

A certain member of the retinue with a steady hand changed the appearance of the year of birth on my passport from 1970 to 1968, which would have made me 22. Passports were not laminated in 1990. It may have passed muster under a neon beer light but I was a little more nervous about the idea of crossing international borders with a doctored travel document. I admit nothing to this day but it's also possible that I had lost track of the duration of my U.S tenure. The passport was a liability and would not be coming with me.

I arrived back at Keith's and got my things together then caught a bus to Denver. I would be spending my last night in Colorado at Ted's who had kindly offered to drive me the airport the next day. We drank a few beers before I boarded the plane and Susan gave me a kiss that seemed to betray genuine affection.

I arrived at Newark at 11.40pm on December 23. There' was nothing I could do but catch a bit of shut eye on the hard concourse and hope to secure a flight to London on Christmas Eve. Using my long khaki coat as a makeshift duvet, I managed to sleep until about 6am.

The Virgin desk opened for business at 9am and I was the first person in line. Presenting my standby ticket, I asked if there were any seats on the next flight to

London. "We have plenty of seats, sir..." said the friendly black lady. Then I dropped the bombshell:

"I lost my passport in Colorado and I think the British consulate is closed for Christmas. Will I still be allowed to fly...?

Less perturbed than I expected, she asked, "Do you have a British birth certificate...?"

I did have a copy of my birth certificate and saw fit to produce it there and then. It was my sole claim to reality. "Ok, I can book you on the flight and you have to take it up with them when you get there..."

I must have had 9 lives but was unsure how many I had used up at this point. I called Dad collect from a pay phone and told him I was homeward bound. Oddly, he was going to spend Yuletide at my Mum's and had a bus to catch. Mum and Derek had split up at the tail end of '89 and so, expecting me home for Christmas, she had extended an invitation to the old man. It was a fine gesture but I'm pretty sure she never meant for him to show up without me. I still had keys for Mount Ararat so I didn't suppose it was a big deal. Against all odds, they put me on the plane. God bless America.

When we hit the tarmac at Gatwick, it was 8.15 am, Christmas Day. To my surprise and relief, customs was a veritable breeze. An absurdly nice gentleman listened to my story before striding off to wherever in order to run a check on my birth certificate. He returned less than 5 minutes later and said I was free to go. It seemed ridiculous that any of this was remotely possible but it wasn't time to celebrate just yet. I still had another 45 miles to negotiate.

The coach driver probably knew that the cheque would bounce like a vintage Hector Camacho but plainly took pity on a young man trying to get home on Jesus' birthday. So he accepted my tender and I was bound for Victoria at the very worst. On any normal day that would have seen me home and dry with Richmond a mere 12 stops on the District Line. But it seemed very unlikely there would be any trains on Christmas Day.

Disembarking at Victoria Coach station 90 minutes later, I took the short walk to the Tube and had my suspicions confirmed. No trains. It was raining whilst blowing a gale and there didn't appear to be any taxis either. The only other person standing at the empty rank was a large gentleman with a Caribbean accent who bemoaned, "This is crazy, Mon...! If mi' knew dis, mi never woulda' come today...." He walked away leaving me without competition.

When a black cab finally pulled up, I didn't even ask the driver if he would accept a cheque. I didn't have a guarantee card but at least I was in the right bloody country this time. If he had a problem then we could discuss it in Richmond, not here in this god awful weather.

With no traffic on the roads, it didn't take long. As we pulled up outside 14 Mount Ararat Rd., I came out with some ruse about only having American dollars and it being easier to write a cheque for the £30 fare. Mr. Cab Driver was ok with that and so I made it out and wished him a Merry Christmas as I stepped out of the car. If it bounced then he knew where I lived.

After nearly 6 months across the pond, Richmond looked so endearingly quaint. I was tired and emotional, scarcely believing that I'd been in Boulder 72 hours ago. Then I put the key in the door and made the most terrible discovery: Dad had put the fucking Chubb lock on...! I only had the regular front door key... How could it be...? To traverse over 4 and a half thousand miles only to be foiled by the anal security measures of one's own blood and kin. I had no option but to knock on the landlord's door.

I pressed the top bell and he appeared in the living room window, half shaven, almost unwilling to process the information before his eyes. Ian Paisley would have been happier to see Gerry Adams at a bring and buy sale. As he opened the window, I attempted to explain my plight. He cut me off:

"Ben, whatever it is, I DON'T want to know. Your Dad's been very quiet without you and I look upon your return with dread, quite frankly...!"

But he was going to let me in, surely...?

"You'll have to give me 5 minutes, I'm shaving and dressing..."

Whatever he was doing it took longer than 5 minutes. It was still raining and a lady who lived across the street was moved to bring me a glass of wine and a mince pie. "Why won't he let you in...?" she wondered.

"He's just not a very nice man," I explained, whist giving due thanks for her kindness.

Eventually, he appeared at the front door and handed me the Chubb lock key. I let myself in the flat then immediately took it back to the uncharitable bastard and tried to sound grateful. Inside now, I threw my trusty blue holdall on the bedroom floor and collapsed on the bed as fatigue flooded my body. Drained but victorious.

I had walked on the Wild Side, surviving lethal doses of LSD, fraternity riots and the petty restrictions of American bureaucracy. I had sung to the adoring masses, mastered a hundred chords and accumulated a thousand phone numbers. There could be no stopping me now.

It was time for a well earned nap......

TO BE CONTINUED....

Please await volume 2 for more Drink, more
Drugs and much more Birds and Boxing

About The Author

  Ben Doughty is a boxing coach, journalist and pundit who resides in Hoxton, East London. Born in Birkenhead in 1970, Ben had 38 amateur fights and dreamed of fistic glory before falling prey to alcohol, recreational drugs and the vagaries of women. These days he tries his best to avoid all three.

His all time heroes are Muhammad Ali and Sugar Ray Leonard. He is blessed with two beautiful sons, Joseph Cassius and Lucas Benjamin Doughty.

Printed in Great Britain
by Amazon